MC

The Adventures of a Maverick Princess

The Adventures of a
Maverick Princess

BARRY EVERINGHAM

BANTAM PRESS

NEW YORK · LONDON · TORONTO · SYDNEY · AUCKLAND

TRANSWORLD PUBLISHERS LTD
61–63 Uxbridge Road, London W5 5SA

TRANSWORLD PUBLISHERS (AUSTRALIA) PTY LTD
26 Harley Crescent, Condell Park, NSW 2200

TRANSWORLD PUBLISHERS (NZ) LTD
Cnr Moselle and Waipareira Aves,
Henderson, Auckland

Published 1985 by Bantam Press,
a division of Transworld Publishers Ltd

Printed in Great Britain
by Butler & Tanner Ltd, Frome and London

For Avril, Dougal and Nancy,
with love.

Contents

List of Illustrations   9

Introduction   11

1 The Beginning   19

2 Marie-Christine in Australia   33

3 Marriage   59

4 Princess Michael   93

5 The Past Returns   115

6 The Princess in Love   131

7 Princess Michael and the Dudleys   153

8 The Future   171

Index   189

List of Illustrations

Between pages 48 and 49

The charm of Princess Michael (Anthony Crickmay/
Camera Press)
Mrs Tom Troubridge (Desmond O'Neill)
The engagement is announced (the *Sun*)
At Wimbledon, their first public appearance (the *Sun*)
The formal wedding photograph (Dmitri Kasterine/
Camera Press)
The wedding ball (the *Sun*)
The christening of Lord Frederick Windsor (the *Sun*)
With Prince Charles and Earl Mountbatten (Tim
Graham/Camera Press)
With the Queen (Syndication International)
With Princess Margaret (Syndication International)
With the Queen Mother and the Princess of Wales (Rex
Features)
A question of keeping up (a: Rex Features; b: Syndication
International)

Between pages 96 and 97

Marie-Christine as a teenager
The royal couple (a: Norman Parkinson/Camera Press;
b: Anthony Crickmay/Camera Press)
The fairytale prince with his princess (David Bailey/
Camera Press)
With one of her beloved Siamese cats (Tim Graham)

An autumn afternoon with the children (Tim Graham)
An unerring sense of occasion (a: Rex Features; b: Tim Graham; c: Rex Features)
In the garden (Norman Parkinson/Camera Press)

Between pages 160 and 161

Princess Michael on her horse, State Occasion (Norman Parkinson/Camera Press)
The family with their pet goats (Norman Parkinson/Camera Press)
Ready for a fancy dress ball (the *Sun*)
Lord and Lady of the Manor (Anthony Crickmay/Camera Press)
Relaxing in Barbados (Richard Young/Rex Features)
With Michael Harfield
Opening a Happy Eater restaurant (Syndication International)
A hat to suit every mood (Syndication International)
The stunning but controversial fortieth birthday portrait (Anthony Crickmay/Camera Press)
Mansion on Turtle Creek, Dallas (*News of the World*)
Princess Michael with Ward Hunt (*Dallas Morning News*)
Hillview Farm, California (*News of the World*)
Princess Michael returning from California (the *Sun*)
Eaton Square (*News of the World*)
Princess Michael leaving hospital (the *Sun*)
At Wimbledon, two days after leaving hospital (the *Sun*)
Aboard the *Jessica* in the Mediterranean
With Jerry Hall and Marie Helvin at a fashion gala (Rex Features)

Introduction

THIS is the life-story of Princess Michael of Kent, born the Baroness von Reibnitz, christened Marie-Christine and called, by some, MC. The most controversial member of the royal family.

She was born under the sign of the goat, and Capricorn women have well-defined goals, which include authority, respect, security and position. The Capricorn woman generally gets what she wants.

Hers is an extraordinary story, beginning in the last catastrophic days of the war in central Europe, moving to the new world, Australia, and then back to the old, where Marie-Christine, thirty-three years old, Catholic and already divorced, managed against all the odds to marry the Queen of England's cousin, Prince Michael of Kent.

Before Marie-Christine came into his life he was sufficiently self-effacing to be known as 'the invisible Prince'. He determinedly backed away from personal publicity. It was not difficult for him to stay out of the limelight; as the younger son of a royal duke, his role in the affairs of the royal family was a small one. If he did not wish to do so, he was not called upon to take part in any official duties.

It was perhaps for this reason that the Queen gave permission for what appeared to be a totally unsuitable marriage.

The Queen has had to come to terms with divorce since the break-up of the marriage between her sister, Princess

Margaret, and photographer Lord Snowdon. Marie-Christine's Catholicism was the bigger problem. Prince Michael had made it clear he was determined on the marriage, and she had made it clear that she was determined not to renounce her religion. The Act of Settlement of 1701 forbids any member of the royal family from either becoming a Catholic or marrying one. The juxtaposition of these two facts meant that, reluctantly, Prince Michael's name would be struck from the order of succession to the throne. But as he was sixteenth on the list that seemed no great problem.

The royal family convinced themselves that the marriage of a minor, if much loved, member of the royal family to an unsuitable bride would be a storm in a teacup that they would weather. The Prince, not being on the civil list as second sons of royal dukes never are, was not obliged to undertake royal engagements. He and his six-foot Austrian/German, Catholic, divorced Baroness would live their own private lives.

What the royal family had not anticipated was Marie-Christine's propensity for self-publicity and her intense ambition. She had no intention of leading a quiet private life. She adored being a princess. She plunged into being royal with an enthusiasm and lack of restraint which appalled the royal family.

They found her obnoxious, were embarrassed by her commercialism and by the way she accepted gifts from wealthy men friends, many of whom in their eyes were socially unacceptable. One of the rigid rules of royalty is that gifts, other than wedding gifts or those proffered on state occasions, are never accepted, regardless of the acceptability of the donor. As Prince and Princess Michael are not on the civil list and receive no money from the State, the royal family could not prevent the Princess taking gifts. They could not, as she is said to have pointed out, have it both ways.

Prince Charles, who had originally felt sorry for her, eventually christened her 'rent-a-princess', which then became 'Rent-a-Kent'. Prince Philip never speaks to her. She is said to remind the Queen Mother of her arch-enemy, the Duchess of Windsor, and Princess Margaret is said to have declared that she will only recognize her when she changes her religion. Princess Margaret's son, Viscount Linley, when asked what he would give his worst enemy, said: 'Dinner with Princess Michael.' The Princess stated that he had eventually apologized. Actually he never did.

The Queen is supposed to have said she was too grand for them, and calls her 'Our Val' (Valkyrie) in reference to the Princess's splendid Wagnerian proportions. An even unkinder nickname is 'BTL' (for 'billiard table legs'). A vendeuse at one of the dress-houses from which the Princess borrows clothes said acidly that the Princess had the biggest legs she had ever seen: 'Fine for climbing. Look where they've got her.'

It is perhaps unfortunate that Princess Michael is so much taller than the other royal ladies and towers over all of them. Princess Diana is the only one who comes anywhere near her height but nowhere near her breadth.

The Princess can't be blamed for her height, but she has no one but herself to blame for her unpopularity with the royal family. There were times when it appeared as if she was taking on more engagements than the rest of the royal family. And the Queen had made it perfectly clear that her services were not required. Working royals are thick on the ground at the present time. They have no need of outside help.

Princess Michael was also unwise enough to say that they would go anywhere for a hot dinner – a remark that has come back to plague her. She also spent the first couple of years of her marriage saying 'Poor Michael needs a job', and touting for work for him. She borrowed clothes and gave the designers publicity by dropping their names. She upset Angus Ogilvy by suggesting she could make the same arrangements for his wife, Princess Alexandra. Another rigid royal rule is that royalty never advertise anything. She made many mistakes and admits it herself, saying she wishes that she had had a mother-in-law to steer her through the intricacies of royal protocol.

The fact remains that the public likes her. She smiles a lot, and looks as if she means it. She is always dressed and groomed as a princess is supposed to be, and she takes a lot of trouble to perform her public engagements with warmth and courtesy. She is rarely grand with real people – only with her own set. And she does have enormous charm.

Defending herself against the 'Princess Pushy' tag that has attached itself to her name, she said: 'As for pushing myself forward, you can't be invisible and six feet tall. I try to wear dull colours most of the time. My husband calls me a "grey mouse" because I always wear grey – grey clothes, shoes, bags and gloves. But when I go to a function, I know I am there to be looked at and I try to make sure for the sake of the charity or organization concerned that everyone enjoys it.'

But, unfortunately, Princess Michael does not only sing for her supper; she expects, most of the time, to be paid for it as well. Having her on a charity board doesn't necessarily mean you get her for free.

But even if 'the family', as she refers to her royal relations, were cool she seemed for a while to be breaking through the barriers. Her husband adored (and still adores) her; her public image was good. She had two beautiful children, two beautiful homes and plenty of rich friends with homes in exotic places so she did not miss out on the jet-set life that she craves. As a young girl she lived in a fantasy world. It must seem to her sometimes as if all her fantasies have come true.

On her fortieth birthday in 1985, the Princess said: 'It is only in the last few years I have come to know myself, and to make use of this knowledge in the most positive way – by looking forwards. At last, perhaps very late in life, I really do trust my own judgement and take my own decisions.'

It was taking her own decisions that caused her downfall. A downfall of such spectacular proportions that her long, purposeful struggle to the top looked finished. There seemed no way that she could not be crumpled back at the bottom again. She would still be a Royal Highness – no one can take that away from her now – but what else? Divorced again? Disgraced? Totally excluded from royal life?

Those who knew Marie-Christine's propensity for survival weren't betting on it. And it looks very much as if they were right. She has come through a series of crushing crises, smiling broadly as ever.

So far.

Perhaps Lewis Carroll was peering into the future and saw MC when he wrote: *she got up and walked about – rather stiffly at first, as she was afraid the crown might come off, but she comforted herself with the thought that there was nobody to see her, 'and if I really am a queen', she said as she sat down again, 'I shall be able to manage it quite well in time.'*

There are many people who kindly helped me with this book. However, they prefer not to be thanked publicly. This is often the case when an unofficial biography is written. I did ask Princess Michael if she would be good enough to receive me so we could discuss her father's past as she understood it. Her Royal Highness replied through her solicitors.

I was dining in Pimlico one evening with my dear

friend, Ann Morrow, and her husband, Gay Fenn Smith, when we came to the conclusion that Marie-Christine's story should be written. By then I knew of her father's past but hadn't done the research which unearthed even more. In the Sydney suburb of Double Bay the Baron's wartime record had been the subject of discussion for many years, and of course certain people in London were aware of it through the poetry of the Earl of Dudley.

Some of the Queen's family were particularly helpful to me. They know who they are and they have my gratitude.

My thanks also to my agent, Dinah Wiener, for her help and support.

Her Royal Highness, Princess Michael of Kent, needs to be thanked as well. She is a fascinating woman who will never be far away from the front pages. Without her, the world would be a poorer place.

Melbourne, Australia,
October 1985   BARRY EVERINGHAM

MC

The Adventures of a Maverick Princess

Chapter 1

The Beginning

WHEN MARIE-CHRISTINE VON REIBNITZ came into the world on 15 January 1945 the Second World War was still raging but the end was in sight. She was born in a hunting-lodge belonging to her Hungarian grandmother, Her Serene Highness Princess Hedwig Windisch-Graetz, on the Princess's estate in the Czechoslovakian spa of Carlsbad. Her mother, Marianna Szapary, was by birth a countess, a devout Catholic and the daughter of the Austrian ambassador to the court of the Russian Tsar in St Petersburg.

Marie-Christine's father, Baron Gunther von Reibnitz, had been born on 9 September 1894 in the small town of Mistiz in the Sudetenland, the much disputed strip of land that was later annexed by Hitler. When he met

Marie-Christine's mother he had already been married to a Margherita Scheer-Tross for ten years. They were divorced after the birth of one child, a girl whom they named Magrit. This half-sister of Marie-Christine now lives in a small town in Illinois and is the wife of a former officer in the United States Army.

Von Reibnitz was an exceedingly handsome man with two great passions: sport – particularly the excitement of the hunt – and the company of beautiful women. As a student in Vienna he had acquired the nickname 'the steiger' – a colloquial word for a philanderer and a flirt.

Unfortunately, he was also a member of the Nazi Party, which he had voluntarily joined as far back as 1930. He became a member of the SS in 1933, the year that Hitler came to power.

At first Hitler's Germany sat lightly on von Reibnitz. He appeared to be of noble, pure Aryan stock, and he thought highly of Hitler's programmes. At the time when the Baron made his decision to become a member of the Nazi Party, survival in Germany did not depend on being seen to support Hitler's causes. It seemed the Baron was not of those whose background could have been suspect and who were forced to embrace Hitler's Third Reich for a safe passage through the perils of modern Germany.

In 1930 when the Baron enthusiastically plunged into Nazism, the officials of the rapidly growing party took new members at their face value. There was little checking of blood-lines and background. In the case of von Reibnitz he was obviously a nobleman with friends in high places. He was in fact the kind of convert that the party, regarded by thinking Germans in the early days as no more than thugs and bullies, needed to give it credibility.

Von Reibnitz's credentials were impeccable. He had served with the 18th Regiment of Dragoons, an élite and conservative German cavalry unit in both the Kaiser's army and in the post-1918 army of the German republic.

He had spent four years as a prisoner of the French, and in 1921 he had formed his own private army 'Freikorps' with the idea of combating the Bolshevik terrorists in Munich. He was a German of the old school. Even with Hitler firmly in power he raised Nazi eyebrows with his apparent inability to remember the Nazi 'Heil Hitler' greeting. He persisted with the old German sportsman's greeting: 'Hail to the Hunter.' His excuse was that old habits died hard.

One of von Reibnitz's highly placed friends was Hermann Goering. They had known each other as young men when they had hunted wild boar together and they belonged to the same hunting club in Berlin. Von Reibnitz was a frequent guest at Goering's vast forest estate east of Berlin.

They met again when Goering returned from Sweden where he had been seeking a cure for his addiction to drugs. Goering, twice married and the father of eight, was a hero of the First World War. He decided he would join the Nazi Party and urged his friend, Gunther, to do the same. They were high-born and both had been decorated in the First World War. Von Reibnitz held an Iron Cross (if only second-class) and was mentioned in dispatches. Goering had been awarded the Pour le Mérite.

Goering felt they could both become important to this new and expanding political party, and how right he was in his own case! He became one of the German High Command. Happily for Marie-Christine, her father's career was less spectacular.

Both men had a paranoid hatred of Marxism, which Hitler had promised to crush. And three years after they became disciples of the Nazi Party the general election of 1933 provided Adolf Hitler with an absolute majority. He became the Chancellor of Germany. By then his political opponents were either in prison or murdered and his party was in complete control of the country. It was in the same year that Gunther von Reibnitz was invited to join the SS – Hitler's dreaded Storm Troopers. His SS number was 66 010.

Historians at Yad Vashem, the institute in Jerusalem which houses the world's most extensive dossiers on the Nazis, are convinced that the Baron was planted in the SS to act as Goering's spy and to be his 'eyes and ears', and that he reported regularly to his powerful friend in Berlin. The SS was formed by Heinrich Himmler, Hitler's police chief. Goering hated Himmler and constantly plotted his downfall.

Yet the four-inch-thick official Nazi dossier on Gunther von Reibnitz which is still held by the Berlin Documentation Centre reveals his only party activity to have been 'electioneering speaking' before the Nazi seizure of power. And his speeches were mainly concerned with the dangers of Bolshevism.

This, too, was one of Hitler's hobby-horses, but the Nazi leader was not yet so murderous in his denunciation of Jews in those early days. The rumblings were there, and the beatings, the house-burnings and the persecutions had begun, but the 'final solution' that led to the appalling deaths of six million Jews was yet to come.

In retrospect it seems strange that both Goering and von Reibnitz were so enthusiastic about the party. Goering had many Jewish friends, but his friend the Baron was in a much more dangerous situation. Von Reibnitz had Jewish blood.

It is possible that right from the start von Reibnitz had felt the cold breath of the anti-Semitism that was to disgrace Germany and believed that to join the party so early would give him some protection.

He was a vain man, dedicated to pleasure, but he was not a fool and he was brave. It was not something that was common knowledge, but his maternal grandfather, Baron Hugo von Eichstedt, had married Ida Crone, the daughter of a wealthy Jewish merchant, in an arranged marriage. In the last century such marriages were common in Germany between impoverished noble families and moneyed Jewish women who agreed to be married in a Christian ceremony – and provide a fat dowry. He spoke of it to those he trusted: men like author Colonel Georg von Konrat, who lived close to the Baron's 2000-acre estate. Von Konrat, who was also a member of the Nazi Party, but who now lives in south London, confirmed that such a marriage had taken place and that was how the family wealth had been secured.

Yet the facts regarding Marie-Christine's maternal great-grandmother were so successfully hidden, perhaps by sheer good luck, that the Nazi Party never did discover that one of its earliest and most distinguished members was one-quarter Jewish. Indeed, so unaware were they that in November 1937, the year the Baron was promoted to the rank of Hauptsturmführer (Captain), he was introduced to the Führer himself and received his commission, personally signed by Hitler.

Gunther von Reibnitz became a Nazi and a member of the SS presumably because he wanted to cover up his own racial background. He might, too, have believed in Hitler's cause. Those of the Baron's class in pre-war Germany had a very real fear of communism, and Hitler's fascism could have seemed the lesser of the two evils. However, when Hitler gained complete control of Germany he began his work of removing from German life all people and influences he considered impure or undesirable. The Jews were at the top of the list. The ruling was that a Jew was anyone with a Jewish or part-Jewish ancestor in the previous six generations. Gunther von Reibnitz qualified on both counts.

Marie-Christine's mother had a different problem with her background. By 1941 when she met the Baron in Carlsbad there was a distrust of the noble old families, most especially those who had not hitched their wagons to Hitler's swastika and still regarded him with contempt as the parvenu housepainter he had once been. Her meeting with Gunther von Reibnitz when they were both in the same hospital was a fortuitous one for her. He was being treated for a heart ailment, which had caused him to be invalided from the Polish front.

The Countess, whose uncle was an orthopaedic surgeon at the hospital, had a compound fracture of the leg acquired while skiing in that winter of 1940-1. She was an internationally known skier and had represented Hungary in the 1936 Olympics. She was also a great society beauty, remarkably good-looking and lively. Her problem was that the Gestapo had been taking an unwelcome interest in her since she had been unwise enough to entertain at one of her Bohemian estates two young Englishmen, one a clergyman and the other William Douglas Home (brother of the former Prime Minister, Lord Home, and now a famous playwright).

The two men had been in Germany attempting to persuade Unity Mitford, Hitler's fanatical English devotee, to return to England before the war broke out. Unity, the daughter of Lord Redesdale, had refused. The two men sent the Countess a postcard describing Unity as 'silly to stay with her boyfriend' – meaning Hitler. The card went through the German censorship system, the Gestapo were outraged by the remark, and as early as 1940 they had opened a file on the Countess. Her passport was stamped 'undesirable'.

Even without the incident of the postcard, the close watch on the Countess was probably frighteningly inevitable because of her aristocratic background. Hitler distrusted Germany's prolific upper crust, while at the same time having a grudging admiration for them. A year later the Gestapo tried to make the Countess leave Germany by refusing her permission to return to her home in

Thiergarten-Heilegen, Bohemia. The estate there had been left to her by her grandfather, Prince Windisch-Graetz, but the area had been annexed by Hitler in 1938.

The beautiful – and extremely rich – twenty-seven-year-old Countess told the tall, blond, blue-eyed, dashing, if middle-aged (he was then forty-seven), Baron of her plight and he told her he had 'connections' in Berlin. He could assist her.

His connections – the Nazi Party and the SS – could not have been more impeccable for the purpose. He advised her that the best way to deal with the problem was to meet the Gestapo face to face in Berlin. He said he could arrange this. 'I was on my crutches and saw a lot of him then,' Princess Michael's mother said in 1985. 'He was very handsome. He wasn't young anymore. He was nearly fifty, but very manly. When something had to be done, he did it.'

A few weeks later, her leg still in plaster, the Countess went to Gestapo headquarters where she faced three interrogators. The Baron was with her. They accused her of harbouring two British secret service agents just before the war began. They were referring to the men who had sent the postcard. The Countess protested that one of them was a clergyman. 'They are the worst,' she was told.

There were other charges against her. She had listened to the BBC, they said, refused to Heil Hitler, and they pointed out that as a member of the aristocracy she was automatically under suspicion. She was becoming more and more frightened. But von Reibnitz, who was enchanted by the beautiful young Countess, had already arranged that she was to become his responsibility. He gave his word to the Gestapo that she would behave and cause them no more trouble. 'They agreed to release me in his care,' Marie-Christine's mother said in 1985. 'He showed enormous courage. What happened then was that the cloud that had been over me came over him, too.'

Having to take regular treatment for his heart condition, he had time on his hands. He did not have to return to his regiment. Soon after the visit to Gestapo headquarters he made his responsibility for the Countess permanent. He asked her to become his wife. She accepted his proposal, but on condition that he rejoined the Catholic church and tried to obtain an annulment of his first marriage. The Baron was not a man to do things by halves and he was very much in love. He agreed, though he knew that if the Nazi Party and, more particularly, the SS discovered that he had embraced the church of Rome he would be in some considerable danger. In Hitler's Germany a soldier's allegiance could only be to the party.

The annulment was not easily forthcoming, nor did the Baron take the final steps to rejoin the Catholic church. Nevertheless, two years after the war began and shortly after they met, they were married in the private chapel in the Carlsbad home of the bride's mother. It was December 1941. And afterwards, though, unlike his wife, he was not a fervent Roman Catholic, he did escort her to church.

The Baron and his Baroness lived a reasonably comfortable life during the war in Breslau in Silesia (now Poland) where he had land and a home, and he was under the patronage of his friend, Field-Marshal Goering. Goering had appointed von Reibnitz as Chief Ranger of the area – the same post he had held before the war – so while Germany fought on widely scattered fronts the Baron continued to enjoy his favourite pastime of hunting.

Breslau was no Sleepy Hollow away from brutalities of Hitler's war. It was an area noted for SS activity and for concentration-camps. Auschwitz was on the edge of the territory. Here the Baron was responsible for a different kind of hunting. His brief was to select and appoint groups of SS soldiers to round up Jews, gypsies, homosexuals and others whom Hitler considered undesirable, for transportation to a concentration-camp. He himself, however, was never personally involved with the camp work. He was also employed in training young soldiers and, as the war went on, the soldiers were very young indeed.

It was against this background that Marie-Christine's brother, Frederick, was born in 1942.

Tortured by the guilt of being married to a man who had been married to another woman for ten years, and with that first wife still living, the Baroness begged her husband to keep his promise to adopt the Catholic faith. Again he reluctantly agreed, but this time he went through with the conversion.

He kept silent about his acceptance of the religion. He told neither the Nazi Party nor the SS, and this deception was to be his downfall.

Trouble began in the winter of 1943-4. The von Reibnitzes had living in their home a woman called Marie Meder. She was employed as a companion to his wife's sister. An elderly spinster and tittle-tattle, she denounced her employers to the Nazi headquarters in Budapest, reporting that they were keeping more chickens than the wartime regulations allowed. They had twenty-eight too many. She alleged the Countess had kept her best skis instead of giving them to the Army, that von Reibnitz had a Swiss bank account containing 29,000 Swiss francs and 100 gold sovereigns, and that they owned three bicycles instead of the regulation two. And, indeed, they had killed a pig at Christmas and kept their meat ration. She accused the Baron of giving hunting permits to Jews and refusing them to prominent Nazis. She also said that he had a solicitor with a part-Jewish wife.

The von Reibnitzes later found out that Frau Meder was a spy, planted by the Gestapo in the bosom of their suspect family.

But the worst damage that Frau Meder did was to send her real employers copies of letters between the Baron and

27

the Baroness, some of which contained scathingly anti-party sentiments. Von Reibnitz referred to Himmler as 'the chicken farmer' as that was what he once had been. The letters also revealed that the Baron had joined the Catholic church and married into it without the party's knowledge.

In an attempt to put matters right von Reibnitz told the Nazi Party that he had become a Catholic merely to please his wife. He was branded as deceitful and a coward by one of his former superiors – a zealous SS man, Obergruppenführer Schmauser – and the matter was referred to Berlin for action.

Husband and wife had to appear before local Gestapo tribunals in Breslau. Von Reibnitz was stripped of his SS rank and his post of Chief Ranger. The Countess was drafted to factory work.

And on 17 August 1944 the von Reibnitz dossier landed on the desk of Reichsführer-SS Heinrich Himmler.

Von Reibnitz tried to bluff it out. He was already attempting to prosecute Marie Meder through the ordinary courts and, being one always to beard the lion in its den, with great courage he went to SS headquarters in Berlin to state his case. He asked permission to fight a duel with Schmauser, the SS man who had called him a coward. It was refused. Hitler had declared duelling illegal. He asked to appeal personally to Himmler on the grounds that he had never concealed his Catholic beliefs on any document or declaration. He added, unconvincingly in the circumstances: 'My loyalty to the party has always been as clear as the sun.'

The SS thought differently. 'The long arm of the Catholic church reaching across the soul of his wife has him in its power as well,' wrote the personnel chief in his report.

Officially, von Reibnitz was on leave; the personnel chief suggested that he should be formally expelled. Himmler himself would have to take the final decision, and in the meantime it was recommended that von Reibnitz be sent to a 'punishment unit' in Russia.

But the report gathered dust. Four months passed in which Himmler had more pressing things to attend to. The war was collapsing on all fronts. The British and the Americans had invaded in the south, the Russians had beaten back the Führer's army on the eastern front, and the battleground was now Germany itself. Himmler took poison, one of the first of the High Command to accept that it was all over for the Third Reich.

In any case, the Baron had not waited for Himmler's verdict. He saved himself from arrest and probably death by persuading his old cavalry unit to take him back. He completely ignored the order to go to the 'punishment unit' where he was earmarked as cannon fodder for the front. He fought his last professional battle as a soldier on the eastern front, against his old enemy the Bolshevik, in January 1945. Colonel Georg von Konrat fought with him. Von Konrat recalls: 'We were together a week, retreating most of the time, and he was behaving like a fool – though some would say a hero. He rode a fine horse at the head of his men. He was like a father to his young men, who were mostly seventeen or eighteen.'

It was the month the Baron was formally expelled from the Nazi Party and the month in which his daughter, Marie-Christine, was born.

The war was coming to an end. Germany was collapsing, and Marie-Christine was not yet four months old when on 8 May the German forces surrendered unconditionally to the Allies.

The end of the war saved von Reibnitz from the fate which overtook so many others whom the German High Command regarded as cowards, traitors or non-believers. He had saved his skin, but the easy life was disappearing for him and his family. The Russians were bludgeoning their way through Germany from the east. The country

29

was leaderless and in despair. The von Reibnitzes decided to call it a day. Leaving behind homes, estates, jewels and many of their heirlooms, they gathered up their children and with a few necessities on a small handcart they fled from the advancing Russian army. They pushed through the forests from Czechoslovakia into American-occupied Bavaria, the baby on top of the handcart. There they found shelter, first in Kitzbühel, then in Altmunster where they had a house and settled while they took stock of their situation.

Their marriage became increasingly shaky after the strains of the past few years. The Baron was already on a wanted list and as a member of the SS would have to face an Allied denazification court.

The Baron had reason to leave behind his old life, and he wanted to become a citrus-fruit farmer in Mozambique, then under the control of the Portuguese but well known to German travellers. His friend Goering's father had been a judge in German South-West Africa, and it was from him that von Reibnitz had heard of this corner of the world where many wanted Nazis were to flee. The Baroness did not want to accompany him to Africa. In 1946 the Baroness divorced him and began to think about her future.

She had a different idea. She decided that Australia would be a safe place for her and her children. She would raise them there, and later, if they wanted to return to Europe, a way would be found.

Years before the war she had met Tom Mitchell, an Australian champion skier, when he was skiing in Austria in 1936. He was married to Elyne Chauvel, the daughter of a famous Australian general of the First World War, Sir Harry Chauvel. Tom Mitchell owned a grazing property in the Riverina district of New South Wales. He had kept up a perfunctory correspondence with Marie-Christine's mother, and it was to him that she wrote when she settled upon Australia. She had no guarantee that he would still be at the same address – but fate was on her side. He replied to her letter, describing the conditions in Australia and saying that, if she wished, he would be pleased to sponsor her and her children, so they need not enter Australia as refugees.

It was 1949 when she set off on the long sea-voyage to Sydney. Marie-Christine was five years old and leaving the old world of Austria to start a new life in a new country.

Thirty-five years were to elapse before her father's past came back to plague her in the most dramatic year of her life.

Chapter 2

Marie-Christine in Australia

AUSTRALIA in the 1950s was a haven for the wretched displaced people of Europe, and the post-war Australian government had embarked on an immigration policy aimed at getting as many as possible to settle there, a half a world away from their war-shattered homelands. Their passages were paid for by the government and they were allotted jobs, usually in factories, as soon as they arrived. In the main these people looking for a new life were housed in disused army camps, called 'migrant hostels', and the conditions under which they lived were primitive. Those who came were referred to as 'New Australians' by the Socialist government of the time. It was an attempt to wipe out the use of the word 'reffo', short for 'refugee', which was used by xenophobic Australians. There were those in Australia who resented and feared the arrivals, who were often discriminated against.

This, though, was not to be Marie-Christine's fate. Aged five she took the long sea-voyage with her mother and her brother as 'sponsored immigrants', courtesy of her mother's old friend from the ski-slopes, Tom Mitchell. Sponsored immigrants did not have to go to the migrant hostels, nor did they need to work in the factories. They were merely required to have a sponsor who would guarantee that for the first year of their stay they would not be a burden on the State. Tom Mitchell had agreed to be responsible for the three von Reibnitzes, which meant that they had to spend a year under his roof. This was federal law. But when the little family arrived Tom Mitchell's wife was pregnant with her first child. She simply could not face sharing her home with a woman and two children she did not know.

Hasty alternative arrangements had been made for the von Reibnitz family to stay with Tom Mitchell's sister, Honor, Mrs Morton Lodge. She was married to a sheep-farmer and they were wealthy like many Australian country people of that time. Wool was selling for £1 a pound, and wheat prices were equally high.

The Lodge family lived at a place called Blowering, near the town of Tumut and not far from Mount Kousciusko on the Australian alps. Blowering had a general store, stock and station agents, a bank and a post office, and that was about all. Today Blowering no longer exists. The valley in which it was situated was flooded to create the giant Snowy Mountains Hydro Electric Project.

But it was to Blowering that one adult and two unsure, confused children arrived in the Lodges' Bentley which had been sent to collect them. It was in this car on the way to the estate that Marie-Christine wet herself. The Baroness was angry with her for letting the side down. Her pants were whipped off and held out of the window to dry.

Blowering was some three hundred miles from Sydney, and a totally different world from the war-ravaged Europe the von Reibnitz family had left behind. Suddenly there was ample food, and no rationing. Though Australia had had rationing throughout the war, it was never a problem in a community where people grew their own vegetables and raised their own meat. The von Reibnitzes could not believe the change in their life. Marie-Christine's mother no doubt missed the culture she had left behind, but here was a place where she could feed her children, where they could ride, swim in the dams, and walk over what was virtually virgin country, and in total safety. And in the winter (June, July and August) there was skiing on some of the best slopes in the world.

Marie-Christine was called 'Vibey' by her family in those days because she was so vibrant. She only had a smattering of English, but soon she became proficient. She played with the children of the tenants and workers on the Lodges' property, but she didn't regularly attend the local school at that time. It was only a one-room affair with one teacher for the twelve or so pupils whose ages ranged from six to eleven. When they were older, they were sent to school in Tumut. It is possible that the Baroness herself taught 'MC', as they also called her, the three Rs.

Marie-Christine was a normal, lively little girl who had one peculiarity. She liked warm ice-cream, and insisted that her mother heat it for her before she ate it.

After the mandatory year with the sponsors, the Baroness had to make a decision about where to go with her children – Melbourne or Sydney. She travelled to Melbourne to see what the town was like, but finally decided on Sydney. She knew Europeans who lived there, and believed it to be a more cosmopolitan city. By then she had already met her future husband – another displaced person, a former Polish diplomat and French war hero, Count Tadeusz Rogala-Koczorowski. He proposed to her, and she accepted. He was a quiet, unobtrusive man, but Marie-Christine always resented him, feeling he did not match up to the hero father she barely remembered. The Count worked as a clerk at Sydney Town Hall, and he and his wife pooled their meagre resources and moved into a working-class suburb called Waverley. It was on this vast human reserve, covering thousands of acres and just two miles east of Sydney, that Marie-Christine was brought up.

A year after the wedding, a son, Mathias, was born, and it was time for Marie-Christine to be educated. The Rogala-Koczorowskis had no money after buying their modest four-bedroom semi-detached house, so the Baroness took in paying guests and bought a small business – a hairdressing salon, which she ran. This provided extra income, and she was able to scrape together enough money to send her daughter to Baratbuan, the infant school at the Rose Bay Convent, whose looming spires the family must have seen on the skyline when they arrived in Sydney Harbour.

When Marie-Christine's Countess mother had married von Reibnitz, a lowly baron, she had dropped in rank: Germany was – and still is – awash with barons. But her children were told as soon as they could understand that their family background was impeccable, and on both sides. Their grandfather on their mother's side had been Emperor Franz Josef's ambassador at the Court of the Tsar. The dubious honour of declaring war on Russia on behalf of the Austro–Hungarian Empire had fallen to him. The Reibnitz side could claim relationship to the kings of Savoy, who once ruled the states that made up Italy.

Marie-Christine was told that she was descended from two queens – Philippa of Portugal and Catherine of Castille – not forgetting a couple of kings of France, Henri II and

36

Henri IV. Attila the Hun also pops up in her family-tree along with John of Gaunt for a little balance.

But, having impressed that on the children, Countess Rogala-Koczorowski had more important business than displaying the family-tree. She also impressed on her children that life was different now. Living in the past was one thing, but surviving in the present was another. She adapted completely to her new life, though she did transform the ordinary little house into a corner of Europe, covering the walls with portraits and pictures, some of them centuries old. She had been able to get some of her treasures out of her home before the Russians arrived but, regardless, the lives of young Frederick, Marie-Christine and their new brother were very different from that which she had known herself as a child.

She insisted that at home the children spoke only French and German. She taught Marie-Christine to cook, to sew and to keep house. There were no servants here. And she was determined that all three should have a good education.

The small Victorian house where they lived had a veranda that faced the green of Centennial Park, which is ringed by Sydney's version of London's Rotten Row. It is here that Sydney riders take their mounts mornings and weekends.

Her mother was also determined that Marie-Christine should learn to ride and, though the lessons were really beyond the family's purse, this was done. She proved to take after her father in being a natural rider, and the ability was to stand her in good stead years later.

After three years at the Rose Bay Convent, Marie-Christine went as a weekly boarder to the Kincoppal Convent, one of Sydney's most exclusive schools. She had become something of a loner, always feeling herself apart from the other children. They were not particularly impressed when she told them she was a baroness and just laughed at her. She preferred the company of her mother and one or two other European friends that they had made. At ten she was a big girl. She was an excellent tennis-player but, though she swam very well, she was too shy of her big legs and hips to spend much time in the water.

At her new boarding school she ventured to be a baroness again, but was so teased that she let the subject drop. It became a joke with the other girls. Also, she was sensitive about the family's simple home, and would never invite any of her better-off schoolfriends to the pretty little house. The fact that she was a baroness, and that the war had cheated her of the life she felt was rightly hers, was never far from her mind. Much of the time she lived in a fantasy world, but she was bright and clever. She shone at school work and was a good pupil, always urged on by her mother. 'We had a lot of "No child of mine ever fails an exam,"' she said in a fortieth-birthday interview. 'I didn't particularly enjoy school. I was a loner, though I do believe in the virtues of a disciplined education.'

In those days, in Sydney, it was not chic to be either foreign or Catholic, which probably caused her feelings of being apart, though she was careful never to advertise either fact when away from her school.

But she grew into a lively teenager, and one who could sew. She made herself the most beautiful clothes. The other girls of her group mostly wore the stretch pants that were fashionable in the early sixties as it was all they could afford. Marie-Christine's skill with a needle put her contemporaries in the shade and cost her little.

She worked in the school holidays at Grahame's Bookshop in Martin Place, which was Sydney's main street at the time. It was quite normal for girls from good schools and good families to get a holiday job in the summer months of December, January and February, though in the main they worked at David Jones, the Sydney equivalent of Harrods. 'The Carolines', as upper-class Sydney girls are called, worked for just three weeks before taking off to the beach-house with their parents for Christmas. Marie-Christine worked the full eight weeks. She had no beach-house to visit.

Author Blanche d'Alpuget recalls working with her in the bookshop during the school holidays:

> She was very cheerful. We were both fifteen. The thing I remember most was that she knew everything about shampoo and then I discovered that her mother had a hairdressing salon. She used to talk about 'singing clean hair'. She was very gay and sweet-natured and somewhat giggly. She was fun and we used to giggle a lot. I always liked her.

Later they went to the same parties together.

> Certainly she was ambitious, but she felt she had been done out of a fortune – which was undoubtedly true.
>
> She was very vulnerable – it was a lot to do with her growing up without a father. And there was a lot of fantasy in her life – she quite liked being called the Baroness, although it was an ambiguous situation because calling her that was a way of taking the mickey out of her. But she enjoyed it nevertheless.

When she left school, Marie-Christine went to work at Grahame's full time. It was a wonderful bookshop, full of exciting titles and very academic. Everyone bought their books there, and she would have found it a great meeting-place. She was becoming a very attractive girl. Dieting had taken care of her weight problem, but she was already very tall with a mass of wild, frizzy dark hair which would stand out all over her head if she did not set it carefully. 'She always had poise, charm and style far beyond her years,' a schoolfriend said. 'She was a knockout socially. When she walked into a party, everything would stop.'

At seventeen Marie-Christine had a way with the boys. She knew instinctively how to talk to a boy as if he were the only man in the world. 'It was amazing how she did it,' the schoolfriend said, 'because at that stage she was a very big girl. To be honest, she was fat. She was nicknamed "the Amazon" by the girls.'

But even then she was socially minded. She wanted to know the right people: the ones who had money, the ones who rode, the ones who could help her succeed socially. There were those who already were noticing that Australia would never be big enough for her.

When her brilliant older brother had to give up going to school because of illness, she shared his Jesuit tutor, and at the end of the Christmas term, 1960, she matriculated, a month short of her sixteenth birthday.

She wanted very much to see her real father again. Her brother Fred had made the trip to Africa, and she planned to go herself as soon as she possibly could. She said she was too young to go to university, but it is more likely she did not wish to go on with her education. According to the Undergraduates Admission Office at the University of Sydney, Marie von Reibnitz sat for the entrance examination in 1960, winning a first-class pass in French (including orals) and second-class passes in English, modern and ancient history, and general mathematics. These passes would have certainly given her a place at the prestigious University had she decided to continue her education.

But instead, aged not yet eighteen, she went to Africa to meet the father she had never known. And he did not know her. On her arrival at Johannesburg airport a young fellow-passenger on Marie-Christine's plane was somewhat taken aback when an elderly gentleman enveloped her in a bear-hug, crying: 'Maria! Maria!'

Once the Baron had sorted out his own daughter from the crowd he took her for what she described as a 'wild-

shopping spree' during their week's stay in South Africa's biggest city.

By the time of her arrival in Africa, her father was married to his fourth wife. He had spent some time in Johannesburg when he first left Europe, working for an insurance company. There he had lived in Killarney suburb, a predominantly Jewish area, and in 1950 had married an Esther Schuette. The marriage lasted only six years, and immediately after she had divorced him he married Rosemary von Buddenbrock and with her moved to her farm in northern Mozambique.

It was not surprising that he had a reputation as a ladies' man among the exiled German community in post-war South Africa, but few there knew of his Nazi background.

Marie-Christine stayed in Mozambique with her father and her stepmother for nearly a year. Back in Australia in July 1963 she talked to a writer from Australian *Woman's Weekly* about her experiences and was rewarded with a full page of the magazine. In those days she called herself Maria-Christina, and at just eighteen years old she had already learned how to promote herself.

The article, 'Girl Goes Hunting Big Game in Africa', was illustrated by a professional glossy portrait of her, dark hair wound high on her head to emphasize her strong-boned beauty. But the long interview has a touch of teenage fantasy about it all. It reads as if that was the way she wanted it to have been. She said that there were several obstacles in the way of getting to know her father again. One of the problems was that he did not speak English and she did not speak German. 'At first, when friends weren't interpreting,' she explained, 'we had to speak in sign language, but I soon picked up enough German for us to talk quite freely.'

Could her father really have spent several years working for an insurance company in Johannesburg without learning at least some English? And was it at all possible that the German-speaking Baroness with her passion for education had let Marie-Christine forget the language of her childhood? Both seem unlikely.

She described her father's farm as a large maize and wheat plantation, though today she says he had a citrus farm. But it was about his second occupation as a white hunter that she waxed lyrical.

> As a white hunter he organizes and supervises expeditions for tourists during the hunting season each year. To safeguard the lives of amateur hunters and to ensure that game preservation laws are obeyed, all safaris have to be led by a white hunter. Big-game hunting is strictly for the wealthy. By the time they pay for their big-game permits, their tents, food porters and the white hunter, an expedition lasting a fortnight costs them at least £900 [a 1962 figure]. The first safari I went on included two American millionaires and their wives and the famous hunter and author, Robert Ruark.

Her 1963 version of events went on to say that there were forty natives to track and drive the game and do all the domestic chores around the camp, and that they travelled in Land-Rovers and trucks. 'We drove inland for two days through lush country with grass so tall that even an elephant could not be seen. And when we reached good hunting country, we saw many different animals, including the hunters' "big five" – lion, leopard, elephant, buffalo and rhino,' she said.

She explained how they lived more or less from day to day on the food they shot, and her father had the rest of the meat smoked to feed his native servants for the rest of the year.

> But we didn't worry about meals while actually hunting. One day when following a buffalo, we set

out at 5 a.m. and did not return to camp until 10 p.m. and in that whole exhausting 17 hours of tension and excitement, we had time only for one snack. But this was an exception. Usually we returned to camp much earlier and spent the evenings around the campfires discussing the day's hunt and singing and dancing to native music.

She also described her one moment of terror while on safari.

One morning I stayed in the camp, exhausted after a hectic day of hunting. It was stifling hot, so I decided to go down to the river for a swim. Cleverly, I thought, I took three boxer dogs for protection, but no sooner was I splashing merrily than some native boys rushed down to the river shouting: 'Menini! Menini!' (Swahili for boss' daughter.)

They had seen some leopards nearby. It seems I would have been safe enough alone as they rarely attack human beings, but they often attack dogs.

If they had chosen to eat one of my bodyguards, I'm sure I would have been made a tasty dessert.

Another and slightly disconcerting anecdote regarding her African stay was the tale she told of how, while she was there, she 'was so poor' that she dyed her hair and her face black and took a 'blacks only' bus to save money.

Soon after her return to Sydney from Mozambique, she told an interviewer that she had spent the early years of her life travelling around Europe with her mother, who she said was then one of Europe's champion skiers. Her mother was indeed one of Europe's champion skiers, but that was in 1936, nine years before Marie-Christine was born. And after her birth Europe was hardly the place for touring. This fantasy world was very much part of her youthful character.

Her recollection of events had changed somewhat by

1985 when she granted a fortieth-birthday interview to British journalist, Anne de Courcy. She spoke then of growing up with the image of a hero-father, a glamorous white-hunter figure who sent wildly extravagant presents. In fact, she met was an old man for whom children were seen and not heard. The period of solitude she then endured was, she says, crucial to her self-development.

> For nine months I saw no one other than my father and stepmother who were busy on the farm most of the time. At night we would play Canasta and I would listen to my sweet stepmother tell stories. I rode, I painted and I read a great deal. I learned to love nature – that's where my interest in gardening began. I don't think I've ever felt so fulfilled within myself or so at peace.

Her own accounts of what she did after her return to Australia vary considerably, but what she did do was to take a job in an advertising agency, and to supplement her income she took in sewing and dressmaking for friends.

The Australia she returned to was a secure, sun-drenched happy land where everyone who wanted a job had one, where the Conservative government of Robert Menzies seemed indestructible, and where Vietnam was beginning to take the horse-racing off the front pages. The Beatles were making a name, and the big bands of yester-year were replaced by groups with ear-splitting electric guitars. The young people were hell-bent on having a good time, Marie-Christine included. They dined at El Capuchino and lunched at the very chic Romano's. Recreation was sailing in Sydney Harbour, skiing on the Australian alps, playing tennis on private courts and swimming in private pools. Marie-Christine wanted it all, and the girl from Waverley got it. She used the time-honoured ploy that all Sydney social climbers adopted: she joined charity committees. The most famous was run by Mrs Marcel Dekyvere, and it was the Black and White Ball committee which raised thousands of pounds (the currency at the time) for the Royal Blind Society of New South Wales. There was a junior committee which the Carolines of those days joined. Their membership was more an excuse to have parties than seriously to attempt to raise money, but they were expected to rally round their mothers when the ball, coinciding with the August racing season in Sydney, took place.

The Black and White was *the* ball of the year. To those to whom such things mattered, it was social suicide not to be there. And Marie-Christine with some courage joined the younger league, without any mother to back her. The Countess might have been titled, but she was not in the financial league of those who were involved in the charity and then she still lived in the unfashionable suburb of Waverley. But because Marie-Christine was fun and soph-isticated her presence among the rich and snobby was accepted without very much question. And she was mixing in the very, very top drawer of Sydney society. All the girls on the junior committee had been educated at Frenscham, Ascham, Kambala and SCEGS (Sydney Church of England Grammar School) – all top Sydney establishments. None, other than Marie-Christine, would have been to Catholic Kincoppal. There were no Cath-olics in that set.

Nor can any of her contemporaries recall her having any great fervour for her faith at that time. If she was away for a weekend in the country, or at Palm Beach, a very swish seaside resort out of Sydney, she did not break away from the group to go to church. In a town where at that time being Catholic meant being working-class (at the very least), she obviously decided it was politic to keep her religion to herself.

She was no Caroline. She was too bright for that. Her mother was still working and there was still no spare cash.

45

She needed a job and so she answered an advertisement for a typist and was accepted by the Sydney office of the giant J. Walter Thompson advertising agency. She was appointed secretary to Marie MacDonald, the agency's home economist.

Marie-Christine was to become part of a team which included Hans von Adlerstein and John Pond, two of the great gentlemen and characters of the Australian advertising industry.

She was particularly friendly with von Adlerstein, who is a German-born baron, like her father, and who also collected wives – in his case, three. During her stay at Thompson's, von Adlerstein was an indefatigable party-goer and -giver, and his waterfront home on Sydney's Oyster Bay was the scene of many get-togethers of the Thompson crowd.

One hot summer's night when the agency crowd were unwinding at his home, Marie-Christine arrived looking ravishing. Her hair was shining, her skin was tanned from the Australian sun, and she was wearing an off-the-shoulder white lace dress. She was immediately surrounded by a group of friends, including von Adlerstein who managed, while she was talking, to unfasten her strapless bra, extricate it from underneath her dress, and hold it up, shouting: 'Voilà!'

According to her former workmates at Thompson's, Marie-Christine was well respected, worked very efficiently, was great fun to have in the office. She also made friends easily with those on the staff. In a word, she was popular.

She seldom refused invitations to their parties, and more often than not she would include them in parties she made up for balls and other charity functions. But what they also recall is that, though she spent many hours being entertained in their homes, she never returned the hospitality. Waverley was an unfashionable suburb, and along with her religion Marie-Christine kept her home background quiet.

Wearing dresses she made for herself, she won 'best-dressed' prizes at the exclusive Black and White Ball. She already had a great deal of style and self-assurance. 'She was great fun,' Sandy Pearce, who escorted her to parties, recalled.

> She was effervescent, beautiful, statuesque, with marvellous green eyes and a skin like satin – potential princess material. The clothes she made for herself were real couture stuff. When she entered a room, heads turned. She wore wonderful jewellery that had belonged to her mother. She was a really nice lady and a good friend.

Others who knew her at the time were not so flattering. 'She was a very ambitious girl and Australia was never going to be big enough for her. She didn't have time for people who weren't going to help her mobility. She was liked more by boys than by girls. She always felt like a Princess,' was a sour comment from one contemporary.

Marie-Christine had already perfected the technique which stands her in good stead even today. She learned the art of self-promotion. If she was attending a function where reporters from the social pages were invited, she would telephone their editors in advance, giving details of who would be in her party and what she would be wearing. Also taking the trouble to provide a few items of harmless gossip ensured a good press and kept her name up front.

By now her friends had taken to calling her 'Schnitzel', but she never mentioned her title once she was older. She was also extremely careful not to compromise herself with men. If she went to balls and parties, she preferred to go in a group or accompanied by two men. There was never any lingering at the front door if she did let anyone take her home to hated Waverley, and if she went away for the weekend with a mixed group she made sure that if there was no single room she was sharing with another woman.

She confided in a friend that there would be time for 'that sort of thing' later. And, in any case, the right man hadn't come along.

The doyen of Sydney's social editors, Mrs Constance Robertson of the *Sydney Morning Herald*, once remarked that Marie-Christine would eventually make the top of the tree: 'She has remarkable style and flair and her ambition knows no bounds.'

It was just after she had left Thompson's that the 'right man' came along. She was devoting most of her time to dressmaking for girlfriends and their mothers, and her handiwork was said by those who gave her orders to be exquisite. She attached Cash's name-tags printed 'Marie-Christine' on to the completed dresses and charged enough to cover her expenses and put some money aside. She was now nineteen and extremely sophisticated for her age. But when she met Ted Albert she became vulnerable, she fell hopelessly in love and threw to the winds all the discretion she had considered so important. The couple's affair was blazingly obvious and it was the talk of the set they moved in. 'Have you heard about Schnitzel and Ted?' was the question on everyone's lips.

Ted Albert was one of the three sons of a prominent Sydney couple, Alexis and Elsa Albert. Alexis, who was knighted in the 1970s, was a millionaire music publisher and his wife, Swedish-born Elsie Lundagren (she became Elsa after many years of marriage), served with great distinction on the charity committees that were so much part of Sydney's social scene in that period. Alexis' father was of German Jewish extraction and had migrated to Australia at the turn of the century. He made a fortune and he built a monstrously vulgar mansion in the smart suburb of Elizabeth Bay and named it Boomerang after the

Above: the engagement is announced

Below: at Wimbledon, their first public appearance

ft: Mrs Tom Troubridge

Above and right: the wedding. The formal photograph shows Marie-Christine's father, Baron von Reibnitz, standing behind Prince Michael; the royal contingent included (from left to right) the Hon. Angus Ogilvy, Princess Anne, Lady Helen Windsor, Earl Mountbatten, Princess Alexandra and the Duke of Kent

Right: Marie-Christine wore a magnificent silk and lace gown to the wedding ball that evening

Above: the christening of Lord Frederick Windsor. Marie-Christine's mother, Countess Marianne Rogala-Koczorowski, is standing on the Queen's right

A member of the royal family
Above: with Princess Margaret
Below: with the Queen Mother and the Princess of Wales,
the only one who comes near her in height

A member of the royal family
Above: with Prince Charles and her 'guardian angel', Earl Mountbatten
Below: with the Queen

A question of keeping up

brand-name of the sheet music and mouth organs which had made his fortune. The house boasted a private cinema and ballroom, magnificent grounds with panoramic views of the harbour, private tennis courts and a swimming-pool.

It was also smothered in the ubiquitous boomerang trademark, and these were too much for the socially ambitious younger Alberts. When they inherited the property, they declined to live in it, preferring their pleasant, comfortable and spacious property in Vaucluse, a sprawling suburb set high on the side of a hill and facing the harbour.

During the Second World War, Alexis Albert met the then Prince Philip Schleswig-Holstein-Sonderberg-Glucksberg of Greece, who was later to become the consort of Queen Elizabeth II. The two men became firm friends and they remain so to this day. Then, in 1951, one year after the von Reibnitzes had arrived to live in Sydney, the then Governor of New South Wales, the distinguished wartime general Sir John Northcott, invited Alexis Albert to be one of his honorary aides-de-camp. With that sort of background and with an eye to the future, the Alberts were very fussy about the company their sons kept. When Mrs Albert heard that Marie-Christine and her Ted were having an affair, she made some enquiries about her son's lady-friend, and did not like what she heard.

She was probably told only half the story. It seems unlikely that she heard the full details of Marie-Christine's background. Had she known that Marie-Christine's cousin, Prince Frederick Windisch-Graetz, was married to her husband's friend Prince Philip's niece, Princess Dorothea of Hesse, and that Dorothea's brother, Prince Karl of Hesse, was married to another of Marie-Christine's cousins, Countess Yvonne Szapary, things might have been different.

All that Mrs Albert heard was that Marie-Christine was

49

a dressmaker, a Roman Catholic and poor with it. To cap it all, she learned that Marie-Christine was an immigrant. 'I will not', said this woman who was herself Swedish-born and married to a first-generation Australian, 'have my son carting around a bloody New Australian.'

Mrs Albert delivered the *coup de grâce*. Ted was told that the affair must end, and he must find a more suitable companion. And an acquaintance of the time says: 'MC never even got to the Alberts' front door.'

For a while, love continued to find a way, usually in the homes of sympathetic friends or during weekends away from Sydney. But Sydney was a small town and people gossiped. Displaying a maturity far beyond her years, Marie-Christine told Ted that the affair must end. Realizing that he would never marry her in open defiance of his parents, she decided to leave him and Australia and seek a new life in Europe. It was where she felt she belonged.

They saw each other for the last time in April 1965 and said their sad farewells. Marie-Christine had booked on the Italian liner *Fairstar*. She had decided at the last moment to try for a berth in the ship after she discovered that a girlfriend, the wife of a Sydney surgeon, was already booked. In her distraught state over the end of her affair, she did not relish the thought of travelling alone. She was lucky enough to get a place in a four-berth cabin, but she was not able to share with her girlfriend.

Fairstar was one of those Italian ships that plied its trade between Australian ports and Naples for many years. It was a favourite with young people because it was one-class, cheap, and formality was kept to the minimum. The officers were Italian, good-looking and out for a good time once they were off duty. The atmosphere in the ship was happy. The weather promised to be good, and as *Fairstar* pulled away from the wharf there was a feeling that a good time was to be had.

But Marie-Christine did not feel the atmosphere. Heart-broken, she left Australia behind, taking with her only a guitar, some valuable pieces of jewellery and her clothing. Her mother had given her letters of introduction to people in Italy and Austria, and alerted her brother, Count Lazlo Szapary, that his niece was on her way. The future waited, but Marie-Christine's friend on the voyage reported that the young Baroness was so unhappy for the first week at sea that she never stopped crying. She didn't want to meet anyone and just stood for hours staring out to sea 'as though she were having second thoughts about leaving'.

The ship went by the usual route: Australian ports, then Colombo in Ceylon, through the Red Sea from Aden and a stop at Suez so that those passengers who wanted to go overland to Port Said could disembark.

Marie-Christine and her friend chose to do this. They wanted to see the Pyramids and the Sphinx and experience the history of Egypt. They hired a dragoman (local guide) in Cairo, who arranged a horse for Marie-Christine and a camel for her friend. Marie-Christine who was always good in the saddle, rode her horse so fast, her long dark hair flying in the wind, that the camels began to become agitated and the dragoman had to ask her to slow down. It wasn't, he explained, that he was worried, but some of the other tourists were afraid that they would be thrown, their mounts were so nervous.

Marie-Christine and her friend were off *Fairstar* for sixteen action-packed hours, and from then on her spirits seemed to soar. She was entertaining the passengers with her guitar, flirting with the officers, and her usual bounce seemed to have returned.

Her broken heart had mended fast in the way young hearts do. And the healing process was complete when, to her delight, she found a good-looking Italian nobleman, the son of one of her mother's friends, who had been

51

dispatched to collect the young Baroness and bring her home. Marie-Christine's companion recalls that he had made a pass at both of them. She said: 'Even if I had been interested, I didn't stand a chance. MC snapped him up and they disappeared. When I saw her again the next day, she was a new woman.'

Her friend bore no grudge. She insists that Marie-Christine is a terrific girl with lots of style, full of zip and bound to get into a bit of trouble. She suggests that Marie-Christine's problems with the royal family are because she is far too intelligent for the rest of them. People tend to be jealous of those who make it.

Marie-Christine was indeed a new woman, on the verge of a new life. After a few days in Italy, she caught a train for Vienna where she was met by her uncle and introduced to Viennese society and to relations she had either forgotten about or didn't know existed.

Although her mother had tried to instil in her daughter that she was a European and not an Australian, Marie-Christine was not prepared for the life of a young woman in Vienna. There was none of the freedom that she had enjoyed in Australia, and although she basked in the time she spent among her titled relations she told friends in Sydney that everything was 'a bit stitched up'. She was just twenty, still not entirely over her first love affair, and some aspects of European life irked her.

And it was not all as she had expected. Her uncle, Count Lazlo Szapary, with whom she was staying, was not rich. He, like her mother, had seen better days and was living in the conservatory of an old house which had become a school. These things were disappointing, but with her sense of the past Marie-Christine gloried in the antiquity of one of Europe's most beautiful cities.

She saw the Opera House, sitting grandly on the Karntnerstrasse where it joins the Opera Ring, and like most visitors she was shown the Rathaus, or Town Hall, where thirteen years later she would marry her second husband. She said to friends that when she went to the Hofburg and Schönbrunn palaces where the Habsburgs held court for centuries she felt as if she had come home.

In a way she had. Many of her ancestors had Habsburg blood and others served the imperial family as courtiers. Prince Frederick Swartzenburg, who is a distant relative of Marie-Christine, tells the story of one of her ancestors who was an ambassador to the Court of the Tsar of Russia in St Petersburg. One of the Tsar's brothers said: 'You Windisch-Graetzes behave as though you are royal or noble'; to which the ambassador replied: 'But, your Royal Highness, we are.'

'Strange,' said the Prince. 'I'd never heard the name until you came here.'

History repeats itself. No one had heard of Baron von Reibnitz and his daughter until Marie-Christine came to Britain. If Australia had not been big enough for her, neither was Austria. She was restless after a few months of the heavy grandeur and stuffy old-world ways of the city. She had finished her crash course in art, and had made a few weekend trips to Paris. Vienna had offered up all that it could for a girl of her ambition. It was time to move on. She decided to try her luck in London, where she would learn to be an interior decorator. With more letters of introduction from her mother as insurance she made her next jump, hopeful of conquering London society.

Little did she know how well she would succeed. It would take thirteen years, and by then everyone would have heard of her.

But what of Australia, the land that had sheltered her and her family and that she had left behind? Once in Britain, she distanced herself from Sydney as she had once distanced herself from the suburb of Waverley and the Roman Catholic church. Australia was rarely mentioned by her, the slight Aussie accent ironed out, exchanged for a slight Continental one. Australia was the past.

But she did go back once, and in vastly different circumstances from her original one-class, one-way cheap crossing to life as a New Australian.

She returned in triumph with her second husband, Prince Michael of Kent, as a guest of the Variety Club of Australia. It was a five-day trip, crowded with events that had been arranged to raise money and create publicity for the Club's Australian activities. Prince Michael was the chairman of the Variety Club's International Life Patron Club for handicapped children and it was 1982, the United Nations year for disabled people.

Long before their arrival, the Princess was on the telephone to old friends in Sydney, saying how she was longing to see them. Locally the telephones ran hot with the news that Schnitzel was coming back, with her husband, the Prince. Her friends were delighted.

There are those who believe that Marie-Christine's experience with Ted Albert and his formidable mother gave her the 'I'll show 'em' attitude that characterizes so much of her behaviour. Now she was certainly showing 'em. Prince and Princess Michael arrived in Sydney on 24 November 1982, on what the locals call the 'Qantas Red-Eye Express', a flight that leaves London late afternoon and arrives at Sydney in the early morning after twenty-eight hours of flying time. She and her husband were met by representatives of the Governor-General of Australia, the Governor of New South Wales, protocol officers of both governments and Variety Club officials. It was quite a turnout.

Following the usual practice when royalty arrives, Customs, health and immigration procedures were waived and the couple were ushered straight to a waiting Rolls-Royce. They were staying at the magnificent Government House in Sydney's Botanical Gardens as guests of the Gov-

54

ernor of New South Wales, Sir James Rowland, and Lady Rowland. Their suite of rooms overlooking Sydney Harbour had been occupied at different times by most of the royal family.

After morning tea with their hosts, the royal couple were shown to their rooms, and the Princess immediately telephoned her mother, and also her closest friend in Australia, Mrs Sophie Wilson, who had already been charged with finding the Princess a hairdresser and making arrangements for a private party where she would introduce her husband to her old friends.

For two people who had spent twenty-eight hours on a plane, it was a horrendous day that lay ahead. The Rowlandses gave an official luncheon for the Prince and Princess in the state dining-room at Government House – a room where the walls are lined with enormous portraits of Prince Michael's royal ancestors. The guests were headed by the premier of New South Wales, Neville Wran, the Archbishop of Sydney, the Chief Justice, admirals, generals and the president of the Variety Club, Graham Mapp, and his wife.

Strangely, Princess Michael's own family were not on the guest list for the official welcoming lunch.

That night the couple attended a dinner given for 400 at Centrepoint Convention Centre, one of Sydney's tallest buildings with sweeping views of the city. Graham Mapp said the evening 'went like a dream'. The Princess shone at this, the first of her variety appearances. She was, he said, almost desperate with tiredness after the flight and the luncheon. She told him she had to keep pinching herself and moving around to stay awake. 'But', he said, 'she was charming and wonderful to everyone she met, which seemed to be most of those present. She's a real trouper. Everyone loved her.'

She was seen at one stage during the evening deep in conversation with Sydney publicist Mick Harfield, whom she introduced to her husband. She had known Harfield during her childhood when he was Father Harfield and he had been her confessor at her old school, Kincoppal. The priest had abandoned God for Mammon.

Graham Mapp recalled that Princess Michael was disappointed to see the site of her old school now occupied by a block of flats. She told him that a piece of her childhood had disappeared – 'like cutting off a finger', she said.

She was at her best for the five days she spent in Sydney. The royal couple presided over the presentation of eight specially constructed coaches for use by handicapped and underprivileged children which the Variety Club had financed. The ceremony took place at the Prince of Wales Hospital at Randwick, and nurses at the hospital were full of praise for the Princess. She toured the wards and stopped to talk to practically every child there, overrunning the allotted time. One nurse said: 'It was very moving to see such a beautiful woman so obviously touched by the plight of the children in the wards. A lot of us had wet eyes.'

She was a success, too, at a charity concert held in the concert hall of the Sydney Opera House. All the artists were presented and there were a good many disabled young people from all Australian States in the audience. The Princess tried to meet them all.

She was less of a success with her own family. Her mother, her stepfather and her half-brother, Mathias, and her older brother, Frederick von Reibnitz, and his wife were entertained to a private lunch in a Sydney restaurant. A few old friends were invited as well. One of them later remarked that it was a stilted affair, and that the Princess seemed quite relieved when it was time to go. Nor did she take her husband to see her old home in Waverley, nor even indeed her mother's new home, now in the more salubrious suburb of Double Bay.

The most informal and perhaps most nostalgic event of

the visit was the launch picnic that the Princess's friends had arranged for her and the Prince. Regrettably the weather was foul, unusual for November in Sydney. The group were forced to remain in the cabin, bobbing on the harbour for most of the cruise, but when the time came to serve lunch the sun broke through in time for the launch to hove to in Vaucluse Bay.

The Princess's family were not invited to this private function, but Ted Albert was. At the Princess's express wish. Her former lover declined. He had, he said, a business meeting to attend. Prince Michael had a touch of *mal de mer* and was green about the gills but kept smiling. Just how, while his wife's old friends were calling her Schnitzel, is hard to imagine.

But a good time was had by all, and afterwards Princess Michael said the party was the nicest thing that had happened to her in years.

Most important, her homecoming was voted a huge success by those who mattered the most and who had paid for the tickets – the Variety Club. When the time came to return, Princess Michael stepped regally on to her aircraft, this time with no tears and no sad songs to sing. She was going, not to an uncertain future, but home to a royal palace.

Chapter 3

Marriage

MARIE-CHRISTINE VON REIBNITZ was twenty years old
when in 1965 she decided to try her luck in London,
putting Australia behind her for ever. What exactly made
her choose London as her resting-place is not known, except that, though she had no money, she did have a formidable list of contacts in Britain – both from friends she
had made in Sydney and from her network of middle-
European relatives.

She told Anne de Courcy in a *Sunday Telegraph* interview
that she came to Britain to study interior design, and that
she was apprenticed to Evie Pinching, a friend of her
mother whose husband was a Norfolk landowner. She said
that when she first arrived in England she used the small
staff quarters in an Eaton Square flat belonging to Evie
Pinching.

'Interior design didn't exist in Austria,' she told Anne de Courcy. 'The taste was Biedermayer, the attitude was "if the rooms were good enough for your grandmother, they're jolly well going to be good enough for you".'

So she studied interior design at the Victoria and Albert Museum and gained a diploma from the Study Centre for the History of Fine and Decorative Arts.

Her friends of the period say that when she lived in a mansion block in Victoria just behind the Army and Navy Stores she completely transformed what was an ordinary flat into something elegant – but not before she had got down on her knees and scrubbed the place within an inch of its life. She was obsessive about cleanliness.

She made black-and-white mattress-ticking furniture-covers and matching curtains herself, painted the walls white and the high ceiling black. Using a portrait of an ancestor as a focal point in the drawing-room, she was home and, as it turned out, to stay.

She kept the transformed flat full of fresh flowers, getting up early to buy them cheaply from the local street-markets.

By 1967, and aged twenty-two, on the strength of her advertising experience in Australia, she was working for Charles Barker, the advertising and publicity agency. Her boss was Reg Valin, now the millionaire chief executive of agents Van Pollen.

He was in need of a secretary, and the Baroness Marie-Christine von Reibnitz was sent for the job by a secretarial agency. She arrived, tall, beautifully dressed, and speaking with a charming Continental accent. In two years her Australian twang had been ironed out – some suggest by elocution lessons. It was the start of a six-month working relationship that ended when Marie-Christine's social life intruded into her working life.

'She worked hard and was fairly punctual,' Valin recalled.

She was good at organizing, meeting people and dealing with them on the telephone. She was very striking and self-assured, but inclined to talk to clients as though she were an executive.

I think that was the trouble, really – she would have been better off being an executive. She was miscast as a secretary.

By now Marie-Christine's social life was very busy. Her list of contacts had paid off. Valin says: 'One night when I wanted her to do something – in our business, sudden rushes occur – she said she couldn't once too often. So we parted.'

She did work briefly for the fashionable interior décor firm, Colefax & Fowler – they took her on as she showed considerable flair for the work – and in 1974 she launched her own business, Szapar Designs.

But a lot was to happen before that. Marie-Christine kept in close touch with her relatives in Austria and visited them whenever she could. They had survived the war better than her own parents, and with them she was able to imagine what her life would have been like had Hitler not lost the war and if her own family's estates had remained intact. Marie-Christine was always conscious of her 'noble' background. She may have felt this birthright was more understood in Europe where there was no longer any real royalty to steal the glory from their masses of petty princes, barons, counts and dukes.

It was, oddly, in Austria that she met Tom Troubridge, her first husband, only to discover that they both lived in London. Tom Troubridge was thirty years old, an Old Etonian, and highly eligible. His father was an admiral, and his mother a Kleinwort of the Kleinwort Benson merchant banking family. Troubridge had chosen banking rather than a service career. He spoke fluent German and had many influential banking friends in Austria. He had flown to Vienna to take part in a wild boar hunt – and that was where he met his future wife. She was twenty-four, very beautiful, very charming. She was also becoming known in her field and was getting commissions to redecorate her friends' houses.

Tom Troubridge introduced her to his family in 1970. He asked his brother, Sir Peter, and his wife to come for drinks at his Chelsea home. They were much impressed. And a year later, on 25 May 1971, Troubridge and Marie-Christine announced their engagement.

They were married on 15 September of that year at Chelsea Old Church – and that time she settled for an Anglican wedding. Whatever the denomination of the church, the wedding was somewhat marred when they had a blazing row in the vestry while signing the register. History does not record what it was over, but it was a foretaste of things to come. The marriage was never much of a success. She was to say later that Troubridge would not give her children. If that were true, it could have been because he had no high hopes of their children having parents who would stay together.

They lived in a house in Gertrude Street on the borders of Chelsea and Fulham, which she redecorated brilliantly – and kept after they separated. They entertained a great deal. Marie-Christine was content enough when she was entertaining. She was a good cook and a good hostess. Her party trick was to take a fresh peach, prick it with a fork and place it in champagne to make it spin.

It is said that Marie-Christine met her first member of the royal family on her wedding day. If so, Prince William of Gloucester witnessed the spat in the vestry. However, after the honeymoon, apparently undismayed by this first impression, he invited them to a shooting party at Barnwell Manor in Northamptonshire, the home of his parents, the Duke and Duchess of Gloucester. And here Mrs Troubridge met her second husband, Prince Michael of Kent. He was, she says, eating sausages at the time.

He was a major in the 11th Hussars (Prince Albert's Own), a bowler-hatted soldier, working for the Intelligence Directorate in Whitehall. Professionally, he had reached a stalemate. In order to obtain promotion he needed active service in Northern Ireland, but for royalty to serve in Northern Ireland was too much of a security risk.

It is said that Princess Michael was originally attracted to Prince William, elder son of the Gloucesters. He was her husband's friend. As boys they had been at Eton together and later went up to Cambridge at the same time. They once drove through Canada together, shooting grizzly bears. They skied and water-skied with Prince Charles's ski instructor, Charles Palmer-Tomkinson. They were good companions.

It was 1971 and Prince William's father, the Duke of Gloucester, was ailing. He was seventy years old; he and the Duke of Windsor were the only remaining children of King George V and Queen Mary. He had suffered a stroke three years previously and completely retired from public life. Prince William had taken over the running of the farms on the Gloucesters' Barnwell Estate. Also, as the first son of a royal duke he had duties to perform in helping the royal family with official engagements.

He had spent two years in Tokyo as commercial attaché to the British embassy, and it was while he was there that he had struck up a friendship with Zsuzui Starkloff, a Hungarian girl. Twice divorced, she was ten years his senior. They were very close, and living in Japan gave him the opportunity to live without the restrictions placed on the royal family on their home territory. They set up home together and were visited by Princess Margaret and Lord Snowdon. Margaret begged him not to contract a hasty and unsuitable marriage.

He took Zsuzui to his home at Barnwell Manor and to the Gloucesters' apartment at Kensington Palace early in 1969. Having seen the impossibility of the situation,

Zsuzui left for America and maintained a discreet silence for three years. She broke the silence in a newspaper interview in which she spoke of Prince William as 'the love of my life'.

The day after the article was published, the Prince was killed taking part in the Goodyear Air Race at Halfpenny Green, near Wolverhampton. An experienced and cautious pilot, he made a bewildering and elementary error. The plane crashed, killing William and his co-pilot. Thirty years old, he was ninth in succession to the throne.

He would have married Zsuzui, had his family encouraged it, but left alone he filled in the years with diplomatic duties and African safaris, and in the summers he took over his ailing father's duties. The year that he and Marie-Christine met he undertook three overseas tours – to the Congo, to Malta and to Liberia where he represented the Queen at President Tubman's funeral.

The new Mrs Troubridge reminded Prince William of Zsuzui, and so he invited her and her husband to the shooting party at Barnwell Manor. It was a great success – particularly for Marie-Christine, who was thrilled to meet the Duchess of Gloucester, William's brother, Prince Richard of Gloucester, and, more significantly, their cousin, Prince Michael of Kent.

Prince Michael was in the throes of ending a tired romance and was fascinated by the tall blonde who spoke with the faintest of foreign accents and was the life and soul of the weekend party. She had been married to Troubridge for only a few months, but warning lights were flashing and Tom Troubridge saw them. Marie-Christine's unconcealed delight at being in royal company made clear her conviction that this was where she rightfully belonged – and where she was going to try to stay.

Prince William undoubtedly found her attractive. He frequently telephoned Tom Troubridge at the Chelsea house in Gertrude Street where they lived and invited himself round for drinks. Marie-Christine would then insist he stayed for supper. She did nothing to discourage the visits – and as a lady who wanted to make her way in high society why should she? The visits became so regular that within certain sections of the family there were fears of a scandal.

Marie-Christine was not the first Australian lady to catch Prince William of Gloucester's eye. He had been madly in love with an Australian heiress, Susan Osborne. Of this romance the family had approved. His mother, Princess Alice, saw Susie as 'acceptable' because she was very rich and came from an impeccable Australian family whom the Gloucesters had known when the Duke had been Governor-General in Australia. She also regarded Susie as being the ideal mother for her grandchildren.

The Duchess was therefore decidedly put out when Susan Osborne, seeing the pressures on royalty, found the thought of becoming a royal duchess so appalling that she broke off the relationship. She eventually returned to Melbourne where she lives with her doctor husband and their three small children. She recalls that when she returned to Australia Marie-Christine, whom she knew, was delighted. The field was clear for the then Mrs Troubridge to give Prince William the solace he required.

William was always wary of single women – and so, for that matter, was his cousin, Michael. Both were conscious that as members of the royal family when they married it had to be for keeps. They felt safe with married women. While encouraging William, Marie-Christine was also summing up Michael. He, too, was becoming a regular at Gertrude Street. Both were content to flirt with Mrs Tom Troubridge, though Mr Troubridge's feelings on the subject are not recorded. In fact, Mr Troubridge finds it difficult to mention his ex-wife at all. But, then, nobody cares for being used as a stepping-stone.

They all spent a lot of time together, and they were in

Brussels when one of Marie-Christine's old friends from the Thompson period in Sydney days spotted her in a restaurant just off the Avenue Louise. Patrick Dougherty, an advertising account executive, and his wife had just ordered their meal and were drinking an aperitif when a statuesque blonde accompanied by three men entered the restaurant. They were greeted effusively by the maître d'hôtel and shown to a nearby table.

Dougherty was puzzled. He said to his wife that if the blonde had been a brunette he would have sworn it was Marie-Christine von Reibnitz, who had been a secretary at Thompson's about seven years ago. He was irritated not to be certain, and finally his wife said why didn't he just go and ask so they could enjoy their meal in peace.

Dougherty went to Marie-Christine's table and, realizing it was her, apologized for interrupting the conversation and said: 'Hello, I'm Patrick Dougherty. We worked together at Thompson's in Sydney. How great to see you again.'

Dougherty was stunned when she stared at him coolly, the famous smile not in place, and said: 'In Australia, you say? Well, that was a long time ago.' She then turned her head and resumed her conversation with one of the men.

Deeply embarrassed, Dougherty was about to return to his wife when one of the men in the party stood up. He introduced Dougherty to Marie-Christine's husband Tom Troubridge, who rose and shook hands. Then the man with the good manners offered his hand to Dougherty and said: 'How do you do, I'm Michael of Kent.'

Marie-Christine gave the impression she was not part of the group. She went on talking to the unidentified third man. Dougherty apologized again for interrupting and returned to his wife confused and hurt. Well known in Sydney for his pleasant nature, he could not understand why Marie-Christine, who had been a close colleague, had found it necessary to be so discourteous.

A short time later, the Troubridge party left the

restaurant, passing Dougherty's table as they did so. Troubridge and Prince Michael said goodnight. Marie-Christine, still attentive to the other man, swept past, ignoring the Doughertys' presence.

Who was the third man? Prince William?

Had Prince William not been in that plane crash, the course of history might have been different. As it was, Prince William died and Marie-Christine and her husband divorced in the summer of 1977. She and Tom Troubridge had not lived together for three and a half years. He had been posted to Bahrain, and though she went there for a while with him she was unhappy, feeling her talents were wasted.

She came back after having redecorated his offices, and left him there alone. They divorced quietly on his return. Yet seven months earlier, when her relationship with Prince Michael was becoming public knowledge, she had said: 'My husband is the most important man in my life. I will do all I can to avoid causing him pain or embarrassment.'

After she remarried she described the day when she and Prince Michael sat next to each other at a luncheon party and both discovered they were emotionally free for the first time since they had met. He had just ended a love affair and she was just ending a marriage. The Prince had had many girlfriends – some like Patricia Wolfson and Davina Phillips he shared with Prince Charles, mostly suitable young women, gossip-column fodder – but he had never come remotely close to marriage.

Marie-Christine said: 'For a long time we cried on each other's shoulders. I saw him, for a year, simply as a friend. Now I'm glad we had that time, because friendship is something you never lose – and when you are in a rocking chair, friendship is what counts.'

She was also attracted by his physical courage. She said: 'I love bravery. He will take on the most terrifying things, not in a daredevil way, but simply refusing to be afraid. Also, I know that here is someone who will always do what is right. If I am in any doubts on an issue, I know his instincts will be right.'

The Prince himself was aware that the relationship that was developing with Mrs Troubridge had its problems. She was still married, but her husband was several thousand miles away and could not be regarded as a chaperon. He took out other girls as a smokescreen. One, the daughter of an actress whom he took away for a weekend, was not amused when she realized that she was being used for this purpose. She heard the Prince on the phone to Marie-Christine, and reported afterwards in tones of deep disgust that he actually called Mrs Troubridge 'Pussy'.

It was in the August of 1984 that Princess Michael gave a remarkably candid interview to Ingrid Seward, editor of *Majesty* magazine – the Bible of all fans of the royals. *Majesty* has a large subscription list of the royals themselves, plus other people who are on the fringes of royalty. The magazine rarely says an unkind word about those who are its bread and butter. However, leaving aside their 'three wise monkeys' attitude to anyone with a title (or perhaps because of it), it is remarkably well informed.

The Princess told Ingrid Seward in some considerable detail the story of her courtship with the eligible young Prince Michael. 'He was a charming spare man I used to invite to dinner parties or when I had extremely eligible European relatives over. I thought, this young man is all alone. I'll produce the right girlfriend for him,' she said. 'I saw myself as a sort of fairy-Godmother, waving my magic wand.'

Majesty recounted that with appealing candour, and amid gales of laughter, Princess Michael told how, with no small risk to life and limb, the Queen's first cousin set out to woo her in the guise of a horseman innocently taking a morning ride.

My husband was never frightfully keen on horses. In fact, after joining a cavalry regiment, he did a compulsory course for six weeks and never rode again, except to meet me in Richmond Park where he knew I rode.

So he went to his sister's house [Princess Alexandra has lived at Thatched House Lodge in Richmond Park since her marriage to the Hon. Angus Ogilvy in 1963] where the Mounted Police use her stables. You see, it is there that any police horse that has a bad record – bites pedestrians or kicks cars – is given its last chance.

Being of an extremely athletic nature and having a secret determination, my husband rode a beast of a horse, which had an unnerving habit of stopping short in the middle of a gallop.

I used to see him and think: 'I know this young man. He isn't keen on riding,' but he was obviously being very conscientious and trying to improve himself. He was always accompanied by a delightful and benign policeman, in case he fell off on his head which, looking at the way he rode, was highly likely.

I thought all this was rather odd, because I never bumped into people out riding as much as I bumped into these two. The strange thing was that my horse had fallen in love with the policeman's horse, and they would be whinnying away at each other through the woods, and that's how my husband knew where I was.

Of course, the penny dropped after a bit, but we literally used to meet like that in the park.

The version of the same story she gave to Anne de Courcy for her fortieth-birthday interview had a little more colour and had changed slightly. She said:

... As luck and Cupid would have it, my beautiful, dancing Anglo-Arab steed fell madly in love with this other rather churlish animal and from miles away would whinny and gallop up to him. Then it was – 'Oh, hello, what a surprise. How nice to see you!' Everything was very tentative at that stage, but I do remember thinking 'He doesn't seem to enjoy riding very much – how strange he should persevere.'

A charming, if flawed, story. Prince Michael is a fine horseman, up to cavalry standards. And the whole truth and nothing but the truth was a fraction more complicated than that.

The story changes when Marie-Christine's friends give their version of events. One tells how she rang to beg off a dinner date: 'I've got a very big fish on the hook, darling,' she confided, 'and I don't want to let him off right now. I'll let you know who it is when I've landed him.'

Diana Villiers, daughter of former British Steel chief, Sir Charles Villiers, moved into the Gertrude Street house with Marie-Christine while Troubridge was in Bahrain. The marriage was not completely at an end, but it had not long to go. Diana, who is now Mrs John Negroponte, wife of America's ambassador to Honduras, tells friends that Marie-Christine fell in love with Prince Michael in 1975 while she was still married to Troubridge.

> While we shared the house in Gertrude Street we would talk about him the way bachelor girls do. She'd ask if he'd telephoned, or if I thought he'd take her out to dinner, or she'd tell me she'd had a wonderful weekend with him. Those kind of remarks.
>
> In the course of the year I shared her home, she fell in love with Prince Michael. Marie-Christine was aware of the difficulties involved. She realized it was enormously complicated and had months of very serious debate with herself.
>
> She was torn between what her heart was telling

her and the difficulties she knew perfectly well lay in front of her. For Marie-Christine it was a year of immense strain. She went through great emotional tensions. She was alone a lot – and lonely. She is not prone to tears, but there were moments when you could see the worry and the exhaustion.

Apart from Prince Michael there were no other men. She had enough problems without adding to them.

Prince Michael, however, was well and truly on the hook by 1977. And those who knew Marie-Christine had been let in on the secret.

The couple were seeing each other regularly. Their favourite restaurant was La Famiglia in Chelsea and, throwing discretion to the winds, they went there frequently. London's Chelsea set were well aware of the new royal romance – as indeed were the gossip-writers.

In an attempt to keep their nights together more private, they travelled by Prince Michael's motorbike, and he was forever being booked when he left the machine outside her house all night. On one occasion, according to William Hickey, the *Daily Express* gossip columnist, it was stolen. But Marie-Christine believed that the helmets they were required to wear by law ensured their anonymity in those courting days.

She says that constitutional problems were far from their minds in those days; they were just two people falling in love. 'We simply did not think of anything else,' she explained.

But, in 1977, Marie-Christine applied to the Roman Catholic church courts to annul the Troubridge marriage. She was on the verge of remarriage to a man whose first cousin was the 'defender of the [Anglican] faith'. She told friends that her conscience would no longer bother her if the marriage were annulled. She also thought that the annulment would make the Queen more favourably dis-

71

posed to her. She did not comprehend that the Anglican church's attitude to the thorny question of divorce is, if anything, more implacable than that of the church of Rome.

There was also the question of the Queen's feelings about divorce. It is something that she genuinely abhors, even though it is certainly not unknown in royal circles. The first member of the royal family to feel the weight of the Queen's displeasure over the breaking up of family life was her cousin, Lord Harewood. In 1967 he was divorced by his wife, the concert pianist, Marion Stein. Almost immediately afterwards he married an Australian girl, Patricia (Bambi) Tuckwell, by whom he already had a child.

He was expelled from the royal inner circle. There were no more invitations to royal weddings, funerals or state occasions, and most certainly not private holidays. He has never been able to restore his standing in the family.

Princess Margaret's divorce from Lord Snowdon was another blow to the Queen, but one she had to weather from her only sister. And, besides, the royal family themselves were too fond of Tony Snowdon to condemn him to an unhappy life. But even with the royal acceptance of Princess Margaret's divorce Marie-Christine felt it would be expedient to seek an annulment.

She was granted this in April 1978, and reverted to her maiden name. The annulment was given without too much fuss. The Roman Catholic church would not have considered Mrs Troubridge properly married as her wedding did not take place under its auspices. Her grounds were that Tom Troubridge refused to give her children. In the normal way the procedure for a Catholic annulment is highly complicated, not to say expensive, with testimony being required from friends and family and from the applicant's spouse. When former spouses refuse to come forward and testify this is the point where many applicants are left high and dry. But the laws of the Catholic church require that the other party be invited to give evidence at any annulment tribunal.

The situation was different in the case of Marie-Christine. A resigned Tom Troubridge finally decided he would break his silence after hearing he had been accused of refusing to give his ex-wife children. He could have said that when they were married the last thing that Marie-Christine wanted was children. He was too much of a gentleman for that. But the idea that Troubridge had refused to allow her the children she 'so desperately wanted' raised eyebrows in her circle of friends. Said one: 'I remember her walking into my place one morning when I had two pre-school-aged children at home. The place was in a mess, the daily help had not arrived and the children had colds and runny noses. Marie-Christine surveyed the scene and before she took off said: "God, how you can have kids is beyond me. I'd die if I had to live like this."'

And yet Diana Negroponte says it was true that Marie-Christine wanted children and her husband didn't. 'She was always very warm and responsive with children,' she said. 'But Tom really wanted to keep his bachelor liberty.'

In New York where Tom Troubridge ran the New York branch of the family business, the Kleinwort Benson merchant bank, he told an English reporter that as far as he was concerned his marriage to Marie-Christine had ended the day their civil divorce (by mutual consent) became absolute. Then he dropped a bombshell. He said he was never asked to give evidence and that officially he was never told that an annulment had been sought.

> I knew about it and I wasn't involved in any way.
> It was a Roman Catholic thing and I don't know
> how Roman Catholics go about these things. I have
> no idea how they got around it or what they did.
> I wasn't consulted and I didn't have to make any

73

statement. In fact, I didn't even know it was happening until someone phoned me up and told me. I certainly was not told officially.

The annulment means nothing to me. I am not involved. No pressure has been put on me in any way. It's nothing to do with me and hasn't been since I was divorced. I never read the British newspapers so it is as difficult for me to understand as anyone else. I don't know what grounds they used or how they went about it. I consider my marriage ended in divorce and by no other means or methods.

Asked about his friendship with Prince Michael, he replied tersely: 'I hardly knew him. Prince William of Gloucester was my friend.'

Marie-Christine, however, told Ingrid Seward:

[Annulment] sounds to some people here like some cosy arrangement that you make with a cheque book. That is not so at all. You have to discuss *very* personal things ... not easy to do, and that is why a lot of people don't even try to get annulments, because they have to discuss things you would barely discuss with your doctor.

Marie-Christine tells how when they accepted the fact that they were in love they visited the late Lord Mountbatten – 'Uncle Dickie' as he was known to all the royal family. She recalled that he said: 'You ought to marry that young man. He's madly in love with you.'

John Barratt, who was Lord Mountbatten's private secretary for some seventeen years, has a different version of events. 'Uncle Dickie' had always been a surrogate father to the Kents since their father, the late Duke of Kent, was killed in a wartime plane crash in 1942. Prince Michael had been only an infant when his father died and he barely remembers him. Lord Mountbatten, who had

74

no sons of his own, had always taken a particular interest in the two boys.

Prince Michael went to him at his country mansion, Broadlands, taking Marie-Christine with him, to ask for advice. He came in great secrecy, and he had come to say that he was madly in love and what should he do? Marie-Christine was both a divorcee and a Catholic, neither of which would be acceptable to the royal family. Prince Michael knew that if he married a Catholic he would have to give up his place in the succession. As he was sixteenth at the time, this was not something to lose a great deal of sleep over.

Mountbatten came to the realistic view that there were two options. He said: 'Either you go and live in sin or you marry. Which', he asked, 'is going to have the worst effect for the monarchy?' Then, answering his own question, he said: 'There is no question. It has to be marriage.'

His view was that Marie-Christine would have been perfectly suitable as a candidate for a royal princess had she not been married before and if her religion had been different. 'After all,' he said, 'she is not a shop-girl. She comes from a good family.' She did indeed. She and Mountbatten were distant relatives.

He was enormously taken by Marie-Christine, who, seeing him as an ally, went out of her way to enchant him. And succeeded. He was their staunch champion against the massed ranks of the rest of the royal family from the day he met her. It was Mountbatten who made Prince Michael do all the right things. He made him write to the Queen and tell her of his wish to marry. He made him talk it over with his elder brother, the Duke of Kent, and with his sister, Princess Alexandra – things that Prince Michael had not been able to summon up the courage to do.

Another bit of good advice that Dickie Mountbatten, their 'good angel', gave them was to stay cool and stay discreet. It was a bit late for the second, but at least today there are no pictures of them together taken before the engagement was announced. Perhaps the motorcycle helmets did the trick.

Lord Mountbatten also tried very hard to make Marie-Christine change her religion, but she wasn't having it. This was curious in the extreme as she had happily gone to the Anglican altar with Tom Troubridge.

Her absolute refusal to bend in any way from the Catholic church is a considerable puzzle. She had little background of churchgoing as a girl in Sydney; and there is always the historical fact that she married the first time in an Anglican church. Why the stubborn refusal to do so again? There are those that say it was an attention-getting ploy; something to make her newsworthy from the start. It could, of course, have been that somewhere between the first and the second marriages she had found her faith again. Who knows? Only Marie-Christine and, presumably, God.

Faced with Marie-Christine's intractability, Mountbatten, who sincerely wanted to help, pulled out all the stops to secure them a church wedding. He talked to the Archbishop of Canterbury, Dr Donald Coggan; he met the Apostolic Delegate, Archbishop Bruno Heim. He had dinner with Basil, Cardinal Hume at the Catholic Archbishop's house adjoining Westminster Cathedral – and he sincerely believed he had won the day. Like Marie-Christine, Mountbatten rarely lost.

He saw himself as a sort of marriage broker within the royal family. His greatest triumph had been marrying off his penniless nephew, Prince Philip of Greece, to the young Princess Elizabeth. And his greatest disappointment was that he never managed to marry his granddaughter, Amanda Knatchbull, to Prince Charles. There are those who say that had he not died so tragically, blown up in Ireland by the IRA, Diana would not be Princess of Wales today.

But his influence was of enormous help. In March, Marie-Christine and the Prince had a private meeting with Dr Coggan, the Archbishop of Canterbury, which fanned the fire of speculation. But a spokesman for the Anglican church did say: 'It is inaccurate to say that the Archbishop has given his blessing to the marriage.'

Eventually, with Lord Mountbatten's help they received the Queen's (some say grudging) permission to marry. This was agreed at a meeting of the Privy Council on 31 May 1978. Four men sat in Council, three Welsh Members of Parliament, Michael Foot, Merlyn Rees, Lord Goronwy-Roberts, and Bob Sheldon, the Financial Secretary to the Treasury. The permission of the Privy Council is necessary for any member of the royal family under the Royal Marriages Act of 1772.

However, after the meeting, the Queen publicly gave her consent to the marriage of Prince Michael of Kent. Amazingly she even granted the divorced Marie-Christine the style and title of 'Her Royal Highness'. This is an honour that is not granted automatically and had been the cause of much speculation in Court circles. Once given, it cannot be rescinded; so, should the Kents' marriage fail, Marie-Christine would retain the title. No doubt it was granted because, whatever her doubts, the Queen did not wish to slight Prince Michael, of whom she is very fond.

Because of the secrecy surrounding the engagement, the Baroness did not see her engagement ring until the day before the engagement was announced. A large diamond and sapphire, it had belonged to the Prince's mother, Princess Marina. While their engagement pictures were being taken, Prince Michael explained how he had stolen one of Marie-Christine's rings to make sure that the ring fitted perfectly.

In the Prince's Chelsea flat where the pictures were being shot, Marie-Christine told of their courtship. 'He was the funniest man I've ever met,' she said. 'From our first meeting, we just kept talking and laughing together.' Then, confusingly, she added: 'I don't think Prince Michael noticed me at all when we first met. He was with such a pretty girl.'

The Prince did not agree. 'I was very struck by this tall Australian lady,' he said, 'very impressed. I remember we had a long talk about the history of art, sitting in a hut eating sausages.'

She confided that they wanted to start a family the minute they were married and said that the children would be brought up in the Anglican faith. But not just so they could keep their royal rights.

> If we minded about Royal rights, Prince Michael would not be marrying me. I think it is a question of who is head of the family, and in this case the head of the family happens to be an Anglican.
>
> I would clearly make an effort to allow my children to understand about my religion and I think Prince Michael would not mind them choosing my religion if they wanted to when they come of age.
>
> I think with this ecumenical spirit it is Christians versus the rest and it doesn't matter which club you belong to.

Prince Michael said: 'I think it will be fair to say that our marriage will cause some controversy, but we are lucky that the Queen has given her consent for us to marry. I like to think she was happy to do so.'

They said that the wedding – a quiet, simple one – would take place in a Roman Catholic church in Vienna, and the following week they flew to Austria to make arrangements. They stayed at the British embassy as guests of the ambassador, Hugh Morgan. But they were counting their chickens before they were hatched. They were anxious to be married in church and, believing all to be well, made arrangements for a white wedding with bridesmaids to take place at Vienna's Schottenkirche on 30 June 1978. It was where both Marie-Christine's grandmother and great-grandmother had been married. Marie-Christine was going to the altar as a reborn virgin. She had, say friends, wiped the entire Tom Troubridge episode out of her mind.

The wedding plans were made in good faith as, apart from Mountbatten's assurances, they had already been given verbal assurance that there would be no problem from the Apostolic Delegate, Bruno Heim. He had been in touch with the Vatican on their behalf before even the engagement was formally announced. It was all a most complicated procedure. Because Prince Michael was a member of the royal family, it was unthinkable that he could become a Catholic; and so, as an Anglican, he was in the position of having to obtain papal dispensation himself if he were to be married in a Catholic church. Nor could he as a member of the royal family be wed in England in a civil ceremony. The Act of Settlement does not permit members of the royal family to be married in a registry office in Great Britain, and that was the reason why the wedding was planned for Vienna.

They were covering similar ground to the former King Edward VIII and his twice-married bride, Wallis Simpson. The king who was never crowned opted for a civil marriage, followed by an Anglican service in a private home in France. They could not be married in an English church because of Mrs Simpson's divorce record. As a registry-office wedding was forbidden to royalty in England, France was their answer to the problem.

Marie-Christine's absolute insistence on the Catholic wedding meant that her husband was removed from the line of succession. Princess Alexandra's children, James and Marina Ogilvy, jumped up one place each, and when Marie-Christine's own children were born they dropped down two.

Then, two weeks before the wedding, the word came that the required dispensation had not been granted by the Vatican owing to the amount of publicity surrounding the case. When the Pope's edict was made public, the couple were shattered. They had believed that the annulment given to Marie-Christine the previous year was sufficient for a church wedding.

But the Pope had reconsidered the matter following the statement, made on Prince Michael's behalf, that any children of the marriage would be raised as Anglicans, even though every effort would be made to give them a full understanding of their mother's religion. For Prince Michael it was a dilemma. He had to promise to bring the children up as Anglicans if the children were to retain their place in the succession. Nor would the Queen, as head of the Church of England, have been able to give permission for the wedding to take place without the guarantee that any children of the union would be raised in the Church of England.

In fact, Westminster Cathedral issued a statement saying that the Pope had found himself unable to satisfy conditions laid down by the Catholic church when asked to celebrate a marriage between one of its members and a Christian of another church. And the Catholic Information Office in London came out in the open and admitted that the religious education and baptism of the children of the union were central to the Vatican's objections.

Marie-Christine, so used to getting her own way, had not reckoned on Pope Paul VI's inflexibility about the religion of children of mixed marriages and, perhaps more important, as a member of the royal family was involved, the Vatican was resolved not to be seen to be bending to diplomatic pressure.

Mountbatten was furious when the Pope finally refused to permit them to be married in a Catholic church. He said to Marie-Christine: 'Change your religion. They've slapped you in the face – you slap them in the face.' But again she refused to listen. And, indeed, if the Princess's religion is important to her, she was quite right to stick to her guns.

The Queen, too, was furious with the Vatican's decision and made sure that the wedding had a good turn-out of royals to support young Michael. Princess Anne flew over with Princess Alexandra and Lady Helen Windsor along with the groom's elder brother, the Duke of Kent, and of course Lord Mountbatten. The marriage took place on 30 June as planned, but in a civil ceremony conducted in German at the Vienna Town Hall.

The Princess tried to stick as far as possible to her original wedding plans. The Vienna Boys Choir had been booked for months, and guests were arriving from all over the world.

It was a funny sort of royal wedding. The groom and his family went first to Vienna's Anglican church where they took part in the morning service. The bride stayed in her hotel room. Marie-Christine's white wedding dress was saved for the wedding-night ball, and she was married in a cream silk suit, designed by the Queen's dressmaker, Hardy Amies, and wore gardenias in her hair. The guests arrived in a fleet of Mercedes, all with the headlights blazing. The bride arrived in a Rolls-Royce, and about half a dozen people clustered around the splendid gates of the Town Hall, wondering what was going on. The groom was ten minutes early. The bride was twelve minutes late, and there was a panic when the couple discovered they had both forgotten their passports, which were needed for the registrar.

An embassy aide dashed back to the British ambassador's residence to find Prince Michael's; and Sir Peter Scott, Prince Michael's monocled private secretary, was dispatched to retrieve the Baroness's from her bedroom at the Schwarzenberg Palace Hotel. The ceremony went ahead, under gold chandeliers, thirty minutes late. 'I think we know who this young couple are,' said the registrar, beaming at the assembled guests, 'so now we can carry on.'

Forty minutes later the Baroness von Reibnitz emerged blinking in the bright Austrian sunshine as Her Royal Highness Princess Michael of Kent.

It was a happy day in spite of all the problems there had been. And Marie-Christine was a beautiful bride. In fact, she radiated such happiness that after the press photographers had taken their pictures they put down their cameras and applauded. The British embassy had a champagne reception for the Prince, followed by dinner for ninety guests, including a contingent of Szapary and Windisch-Graetz relations. Marie-Christine's mother had flown in from Australia, and her father flew in from Mozambique. It was the first time he had seen his ex-wife since 1948 and his daughter since 1962. Not surprisingly, he kept a low profile at the wedding. In fact, most of the press who covered the event had no idea he was there. And, at the wedding ball at the Schwarzenberg Palace, Marie-Christine wore the magnificent silk and lace gown that she had planned to wear at a church wedding. In the Viennese tradition the newlyweds opened the dancing to Lehar's 'Gold and Silver Waltz'. Marie-Christine said afterwards that 'Michael never really got over the dizzying speed of the waltz, but it started our adventure in life together'.

Their civil marriage was not recognized by the church, so the couple had agreed to spend their wedding night apart. This enabled Marie-Christine to attend a private mass the next morning to bless her union in the monastery church where she had planned to be married. It seemed like a charming gesture, even if most of those at the wedding must have been hard put to believe that her relationship had not already been consummated. And, if that were the case, the dramatic gesture of the wedding night spent apart was more than a touch hypocritical.

The brand new Princess could not take holy communion if the marriage were consummated, for in the eyes of her church she was living in sin. And a spokesman on Roman Catholic law said: 'The Baroness seems to be taking advantage of a technical loophole. The fact that she has not consummated her civil marriage is being used as a pretext for taking Holy Communion. Most Catholics would regard her reception of Holy Communion in these circumstances as highly inappropriate.'

The church spokesman added that the civil marriage ceremony was not recognized by the Roman Catholic church. The 'irregular union' – the modern phraseology for living in sin – would not begin until the couple had consummated their marriage. After that, the Princess would be barred from taking Holy Communion.

It was a situation that caused the kind-hearted Prince Charles to say at a Salvation Army congress that same day that Christians were bogged down over religious dogma 'which can only bring needless distress to people'. Having congratulated the Salvation Army for what he called an unfettered brand of Christianity he found his remarks were not so popular with the established churches. Buckingham Palace hastily said that the timing of Prince Charles's remarks was purely coincidental.

While Prince Charles was receiving an ecclesiastical rap over the knuckles, Prince Michael and his new bride were setting off on their honeymoon which took in India, Iran and Paris. It was in Paris that they visited the Duchess of Windsor – the American woman who was the sole cause of Edward VIII's abdication.

The Duchess, once Mrs Wallis Warfield Simpson, was by then eighty-two, senile, and a prisoner of failing health in her Parisian home. The visit cannot have been very rewarding, but Princess Michael is fascinated by the

Duchess and her story, perhaps because she sees some parallels with her own history. There is no true comparison. Edward VIII gave up the crown for the woman he loved. Prince Michael gave up his sixteenth place in the succession. Short of a plague wiping out most of the royal family, his wife would have had little chance of finding herself the first divorced woman to be Queen of England. In truth, the Princess has been treated more kindly by the Establishment than ever the Duchess of Windsor was. In her entire lifetime the ex-King's wife was never permitted to call herself Royal Highness. She had been married twice already, and the royal family feared that her marriage with Edward might not last, either.

One wonders what Prince Michael's mother would have thought about it all. Marina, the stunningly elegant Greek princess who married George, Duke of Kent, was a royal of the old school. After her husband was killed at the age of forty in the course of his wartime duties she was always desperately short of money, yet she managed to live and bring up her three children with dignity and without ever resorting to the commercialism which occupies so many of Princess Michael's waking hours.

Marina's attitude was unshakeable. If her children were to marry outside the royal circle, it should be to people with impeccable family backgrounds and whose religion and education were suitable to a member of the world's greatest royal dynasty. And she wasn't too content about the choices of her two eldest.

When Eddie, the Duke of Kent, starting courting Katherine Worsley, Princess Marina heard warning bells and she moved in quickly to nip in the bud what she believed to be an unsuitable marriage. Eddie was only twenty-one and Kate two years his senior. She was not royal in any way.

Katherine had a copy-book English county background and had never been involved in the slightest hint of scandal. Her father, Sir William Worsley, was Lord Lieutenant of Yorkshire's North Riding. His home near York, Hovingham Hall, is a late eighteenth-century manor-house filled with fine antiques.

Had Eddie's regiment not been posted to Catterick in the North Riding he would never have met his wife. He hated the thought of being so far from London, and his aunt the Princess Royal and his sister, Alexandra, introduced him to people who lived in the area. But Eddie met Katherine through her father, who was given to inviting officers from the camp to Sunday lunch.

Eddie began courting Katherine, but did not tell his mother. She first knew when Eddie told her he was going to ask the Queen if he could be excused from the royal family's Christmas festivities and go to Hovingham Hall instead. Princess Marina was dismayed. She said the Queen would never agree, and in any case he wasn't to ask. He did ask, and the Queen said 'yes'. He had told her he was in love.

Marina checked out the Worsleys and found that her son was involved with a girl whose background, though not royal, was certainly old, with roots going back to the eleventh century. But she was still not delighted, and was probably also affronted when Katherine, as much in love as she was, unsure of the pressures of being royal, hesitated before accepting the Duke's proposal.

Princess Marina would have liked her daughter Alexandra to have married a European prince. Instead she chose Angus Ogilvy, a man eight years her senior and the second son of the Earl of Airlie. The Airlies have a long history of royal service, and indeed it was Angus's older brother, the present Earl, who was asked to check on Marie-Christine's background when it was known that she and Prince Michael were more than just good friends.

As it turned out, Marina's older children have had happy marriages, producing five children between them.

Princess Marina did not live to see her grandchildren mature, nor to see the choice of bride her favourite, Michael, made.

The idea of her youngest son marrying a divorced woman in a civil ceremony in a foreign country would have appalled her. In fact, had Princess Marina not died in 1968, it is unlikely that the marriage would have taken place.

It was she and the present Queen Mother who, after Queen Mary, were the most implacably opposed to the marriage between Wallis Simpson and Edward VIII. It was that same year, 1936, that Prince Michael's older sister, Princess Alexandra, was born on Christmas Day and Queen Mary, the King's mother, said it was the nicest thing that had happened that year.

The Kents were never rich by royal standards and they leased a house in London's Belgravia. Soon after their son, Eddie, now Duke of Kent, was born, the Duchess inherited Coppins, a country house near Iver in Buckinghamshire. She lived there as wife, widow and mother until she gave the house to her elder son when he married Katherine Worsley. From then until her death, she lived in a grace-and-favour apartment in Kensington Palace with Prince Michael, just as Prince Michael and his wife do today.

Michael was a wartime baby, born at Coppins on 4 July 1942. His father, a serving officer in the RAF, was on leave for the birth. It was as if he had a premonition that he would not survive to enjoy the baby for long, for he spent as much time as he could in the nursery with Michael, leaving the dinner-table early to be with his baby son before he went to sleep. Soon after his birth, Michael was taken to Windsor Castle where he was christened Michael George Charles Franklin. Franklin D. Roosevelt, President of the United States, was a godfather.

Three weeks later, Michael's father said goodbye to his

family and flew off to Iceland on a tour of inspection. His plane crashed into a mountainside in Scotland, leaving behind a numbed and grieving family. The wartime Prime Minister, Winston Churchill, said that the loss of the Duke of Kent, so gallant and so handsome, in the prime of his life had been a shock and sorrow to the people of the British Empire, standing out lamentably even in the hard days of war. And it was true. The British did grieve with Princess Marina and her children, and for ever afterwards she was the public's darling.

Princess Marina, a foreigner in Britain all her life, would have been hard put to understand Princess Michael's assertion that the British public would have preferred Prince Michael to take an English wife. When Ingrid Seward raised this point Marie-Christine explained:

> Not so much just an English wife, but if he had to choose a foreigner, why did she have to be Catholic and divorced?
>
> I don't know about the public, because I think the public is very generous and rather wonderful and don't mind as long as their princes or princesses are happy, but I think there was a certain section of society that said: 'wasn't one of our girls good enough for him? Why did he have to look abroad for a wife?'
>
> I was totally misquoted when I tried to make this point and I would like to make it here because it is something that helped me rationalize my position, especially in the beginning. If the opposite situation had occurred and an English girl, Anglican, Protestant, divorced, had gone to Austria and married into one of our Archducal families, don't think that Austrian society would have been pleased. It would not have been a marriage received with open arms at all, because we are much stricter in a funny sort of way.
>
> I think this is a very valid point to make because

87

I wasn't received with open arms in some sections of society, but I know my own family's reaction would have been: 'Oh! We wish he had chosen one of our girls.' So bearing that in mind, I accept that I wasn't perhaps the most ideal choice.

This woman who was brought up from the age of five in Australia, went to Australian schools and who has only lived in central Europe for the shortest possible time has an obsession about what she calls her foreignness.

She said to writer Anne de Courcy in her fortieth-birthday interview:

From the beginning I realized people would be against me. I'm foreign, divorced, Catholic – all the things rolled into one that even individually tolerant members of the Royal family don't want to see in the Royal family.

The whole key to me is my foreignness. But because I talk English like an English person, have English colouring and lead a very English life, subconsciously people expect me to be English in every way. But I'm not. I'm as foreign as could be and being foreign means thinking differently, having different values, getting excited about different things. English people, for example, tend to retain a diffident manner even when they are really not shy or unconfident – foreigners don't. And I am central European through and through.

Well, Marie-Christine certainly has all the survival instincts of the central Europeans.

For one thing, she was not going to let the Catholic church get away with it. For the next five years after her marriage, she devoted much of her time and energy to reversing the Pope's ban against her church wedding. It became an obsession, lobbying through lawyers and intervening personally in the delicate negotiations without cease until finally she won.

On 27 July 1983 it was announced that the Holy See had agreed to recognize the marriage of Prince and Princess Michael of Kent. By then Princess Michael, confident that victory was hers, had made arrangements for her 'second marriage' and was furious when her plans were leaked before she had the Pope's official approval. When she received his approval by telex from Rome she made hurried moves to speed up the private ceremony.

On 30 July, five years after the Vienna civil ceremony, Marie-Christine had her church service – a blessing – and was accepted back into her own church, at Cardinal Hume's private chapel at Westminster.

This time she had a larger audience. About 300 people were waiting to greet the royal couple as they left the Cardinal's residence afterwards. The Princess wore the same cream suit she had worn for the Town Hall wedding in Vienna and carried a small posy of flowers. The Prince wore a pin-striped suit with a yellow rose in his buttonhole. Though the priest did not perform a marriage ceremony, he included many of the vows and rituals of the traditional marriage. The Prince and Princess exchanged the same rings they used when they were first married and, though they did not promise to 'honour and obey', the Princess firmly repeated the words 'to love and to cherish till death us do part'.

The chief witnesses, the Duke of Kent and Princess Alexandra, looked on, standing only a few feet behind the couple as they knelt in front of the grey marble altar of the tiny chapel, a room which is normally used as the private chapel of Cardinal Hume. He, perhaps fortuitously as the Pope's change of mind did not find favour with all Catholics, was away on holiday. The Apostolic Nuncio, Bruno Heim, the Vatican representative in London, was recovering from a major operation, so Monsignor Ralph Brown, the chief officiator at weddings in Westminster Cathedral, stood in. The royal party signed the register before being offered a celebratory glass of champagne by Monsignor Brown.

And he was remarkably chatty after the event. He spoke of a moment of emotion that a priest would not find strange, but: 'It was clearly there,' he said. 'I felt that it occurred today. It wasn't said, but it was implied that the prince and princess felt this was a special day for both of them. This was different.'

After the royal couple had left, he elaborated further. 'There were very few people there,' he said. 'The couple, the two witnesses, myself and two assistant priests. Everyone preferred that it remained private. During the ceremony the royal couple exchanged rings – which had been blessed – and took the vows again. There were readings from the Song of Solomon, First Corinthians on charity and the Sermon on the Mount. The couple chose the readings themselves.'

As it happened, the couple spent both their wedding nights apart. When dusk fell on their second marriage, Prince Michael was already at a lively party at the Corinthian Club in Cowes where he planned to spend most of Cowes week as guest of Lord Montagu of Beaulieu. The Princess was at home in Kensington Palace. She dislikes small boats and sailing.

There were already rumblings in the Catholic church about the significance of the event. The Roman Catholic newspaper, *The Universe*, said that this 'marriage' looked unfair to those who, in order to remain loyal to the laws of the church, turn down a chance of marriage when their prospective partner refused to bring up the children in the Catholic church. It called upon Pope John Paul II for an explanation, pointing out that he had reversed an earlier ruling by Pope Paul VI. It went on to say:

> Obviously the Pope, who is extremely open and
> firm in defending the sanctity of marriage, must

have good reason for granting the Princess's request now.

But in order to avoid confusion and scandal it is not enough for justice to be done, it must also be seen to be done. Catholics have a right to a public explanation.

They received one when the Catholic Information Office issued a press statement saying that in 1971 the Holy See made it possible for a bishop to give permission for mixed marriages to take place in another Christian church. 'Clearly,' the statement said, 'over a period of years Princess Michael must have satisfied the Church authorities that she is doing all in her power to bring her children up in the knowledge and love of the faith.'

Was the annulment 'arranged'? It is a suggestion that enrages the Princess. 'I do not see why people question it, as though it was granted just because I wanted to marry a Prince,' she has said. 'It was all right, legitimate, absolutely within Catholic law. Tom would not give me children and that invalidated the marriage.'

The Princess herself does not have an unfettered brand of Christianity. In spite of the promise to bring up the two children she now has as Anglicans, she bends the rules. She openly states that she takes the children to her own church every other week. And she has put Lord Frederick down for Eton in 1992 where he will go to the house run by Dr Michael Atkinson, who will, by then, be Eton's first Roman Catholic housemaster.

In 1983 the same Monsignor Brown said that the Kent children could become Catholic because of their mother's influence. The Monsignor went on to say that there were many ways in which a Catholic mother in a mixed marriage could influence young children by teaching them prayers and helping them make the sign of the cross. In due time when the children were old enough they would be in a position to make their own decisions.

The point that he missed was that, if the children do decide to adopt their mother's religion, like their father they will have to relinquish their right of succession to the throne. Father Brown's statement met with deafening silence from Buckingham Palace, but Princess Michael's friends had been saying privately for some time that she would, when the time was right, lobby tame Members of Parliament to see if the Act of Settlement could be changed so that Catholics could succeed. This would mean that Prince Michael could be reinstated.

But, once again, the Princess failed to understand the underpinnings of the British monarchy. Even in these ecumenically minded days, the truth is that she hasn't a chance.

Chapter 4

Princess Michael

THE FIRST SNAG to hit Marie-Christine's royal marriage was the age-old one of money. There wasn't enough of it, and the Princess spends a lot of it.

The Prince lived in a small flat in Chelsea. He was not, and is not, a wealthy man. When his mother, Princess Marina, died she left a relatively small amount to be shared between her three children, the Duke of Kent, Princess Alexandra and the baby of the family, Prince Michael. The story that Lord Mountbatten had willed Prince Michael a quarter of a million pounds is not true. Lord Mountbatten left £3 million and he left it to his own family. The Prince had received small bequests from his grandfather, King George V, and his uncle, George VI, but by royal standards he was not financially well endowed and his financial prospects did not look good. He was neither well paid at around £7500 a year, nor happy in the Army where he had spent nearly twenty years of his life. He was a major and he had just been offered a job in the Ministry of Defence Intelligence Directorate. In two years he would become a lieutenant-colonel, and after that his chances of promotion were slight. His new Princess considered his salary to be totally inadequate for their life-style. Michael, she decided, was going to have to get a proper, well-paid job or get himself on the civil list.

The point that she could not grasp – and, indeed, may still not have grasped – is that Michael is not entitled to any portion of the Queen's civil list. This is the annual sum – around £4.5 million – which the State pays the Queen to run the monarchy and which she doles out in varying amounts to her relatives who are entitled to a share. As the second son of a royal duke, Prince Michael does not qualify. The rules are the rules, but this particular rule Princess Michael believes to be desperately unfair.

If Marie-Christine wanted, as she did, to get on the royal roundabout and play the Princess, then she and her husband were going to have to pay for the pleasure out of their own pocket, or someone was going to have to pay them secretly for doing it. But that someone would definitely not be the Queen or the British taxpayer.

They had one stroke of luck, which came about because the Queen is extremely fond of Prince Michael. When they returned from honeymoon it was to the news that the Queen had decided to give them a reception at St James's Palace; but, even better, she was also giving them a grace-and-favour apartment at Kensington Palace, next door to where the Prince and Princess of Wales later came to live. It was the house that Princess Margaret and Anthony Armstrong Jones used when they were first married. There are eight bedrooms, a floor for the children, one floor for the Prince and Princess, one floor of receiving-rooms, and a huge amount of office space. They pay no rent and repair bills. These are looked after by the Department of the Environment. They do have to pay the rates, which are not inconsiderable.

Their house in the country, Nether Lypiatt Manor, set in thirty-five acres near Stroud in Gloucestershire, cost £300,000, and where that sort of money came from has been very much open to debate from the day that they bought it. The Princess denied that it was paid for by a bequest from Mountbatten – 'Would that he had left us the money!' she said. But she did not give any indication of how the house was paid for other than telling a whimsical story about how the house's resident ghost took a shine to her. It seems the ghost was so keen for her to live at the Manor that it saw off the three higher bidders for the property. Two died and one went bankrupt.

Nether Lypiatt Manor is their own financial problem. Prince Michael's salary is reckoned to be in the region of £40,000 a year (and he, unlike the Queen, pays normal income tax). He has four directorships, one with Standard Telegraph and Cables, one with Aitken Hume, one with Walbrook Investments and the fourth with London United Investments, a big City insurance group. It is no wonder that the Princess has to run both the houses with only a housekeeper and two efficient daily women, a girl groom and a gardener. When she needs staff for one of her parties she borrows from Buckingham Palace. She rings the Head Steward at Buckingham Palace, asks if anyone who is off-duty would like to oblige, and then herself pays the Queen's footmen, chefs, etc., the going rate for the job. She does a great deal herself about the house. During a broadcast in 1984, she confessed that her husband calls her 'Mrs Ogmore-Prichard', because she is so tidy – as was the character of that name in Dylan Thomas's *Under Milk Wood*.

When Prince Michael was in the Army, his salary was much less than what he earns for his directorships today, and even before they were married the Princess was trying to find him a post. She had a friend whose husband was a member of a City partnership and with whom she had spent several holidays at their home in Tuscany. Marie-Christine telephoned the wife and suggested that she and her husband dine with Michael and her at his flat in Cheyne Walk one night. She herself was still living in the Troubridge matrimonial home in Gertrude Street then but she preferred entertaining in Michael's apartment. Her friends accepted the invitation. Marie-Christine then explained that the evening would be quite informal. There would just be the four of them for dinner and she would be doing the cooking.

The couple arrived and were presented to the Prince. Marie-Christine served a superb dinner, and the after-dinner subject was Prince Michael's career. After much discussion, an appointment was made for the Prince to meet some City men who were on various boards and might be of some help. The evening was a success. Marie-Christine's friends were very taken with the Prince, whom they found charming and friendly. They were also pleased that they had been able to help, and that she had seemed so happy with the outcome of the evening.

Their pleasure turned to dismay when Marie-Christine telephoned the next day to complain that they were far too familiar with Prince Michael. Then came the warning that if they wanted to be on her visiting-list after she became royal they had better learn how to behave in the presence of royalty.

It was the first touch of the *folie de grandeur* that was to cause so much of the Princess's unpopularity. Right from the beginning she made unwise remarks about how she loved being royal, how she could hardly wait to be asked to plant trees, open fêtes and head a regiment. Her eager-

The early years in Australia – Marie-Christine as a teenager

Above and below: the royal couple

Right: the fairytale Prince with his Princess

Above: with one of her beloved Siamese cats
Right: enjoying Ascot
Below: an intimate moment

An unerring sense of occasion

n autumn afternoon with the children

ness to be royal has led her into accepting engagements that the rest of the royal family would not touch. In April 1985, for example, she had three engagements: a Metropolitan Police Division luncheon in Essex, the opening of a fast-food restaurant in Surrey, and the Doctor of the Year lunch in London. Her husband had only one engagement: visiting the headquarters of the Institute of Marketing at Cookham. She irritates her in-laws by creating royal functions where there are none, as she did when she turned up at David Bowie's return to his Brixton home to open a youth centre.

John Barratt, who worked as the Prince and Princess's secretary soon after their marriage, explained how the public appearances were originally Lord Mountbatten's idea. Mountbatten agreed with Marie-Christine that the Prince should leave the Army and get a job. 'Why not start to undertake a few engagements?' he said 'Get yourself known, and then you might get some offers.'

It was a sensible suggestion. The Prince had been virtually faceless before he became involved with Marie-Christine. His anonymity was something of a family joke, so much so that when Marie-Christine was introduced to Princess Margaret's young son, Viscount Linley, as Prince Michael's future bride, Linley said: 'Prince Michael? Which one's he?'

Marie-Christine was both infuriated and mortified. She made up her mind to put her future husband in the limelight – somewhere, if the truth were told, he would probably rather not be.

But they took Mountbatten's advice, and the engagements that were meant to be a means to an end multiplied. And it all backfired. Princess Michael became a public figure. 'The idea was to get people to employ the husband, but the result is that people began to ask if they could employ the wife,' John Barratt, their ex-secretary, said.

He recalls going to one of their first engagements with Lord Mountbatten and being amazed at how easily Princess Michael coped with the unfamiliar situation. 'She is', said Lord Mountbatten gleefully, 'a natural.' Mountbatten was convinced that channelled in the right direction the Princess could become a real asset to the royal family.

It was not long after he had left the Kents' employment three years ago (May 1983) that John Barratt said:

> Bearing in mind their position, the Kents still aren't on easy street. As the Prince is not on the civil list he cannot use the Queen's flight. Therefore, when long-distance engagements were suggested when I was working for them, we had to do a lot of sums. We had to work out if they could fit in two or three appearances for the price of one air flight or train journey.
>
> It was a question of juggling finances, because royalty most certainly do not get paid for appearances, whether they are on the civil list or not.
>
> They [the Kents] have to accept things that don't involve them in too much expense. Long train journeys are out because of the fares, and they are really not supposed to accept their expenses. Officially, the Queen said that she did not require her cousin, Michael, to carry out royal duties. They have no need to do so. They can take whatever engagements they like, but there will be no official cars to transport them, nor Government money to pay for staff.
>
> They have a very small staff. The Princess has a part-time maid. Fortunately she is particularly good at doing her own hair and she dresses herself exceptionally well – with a little help from her friends in the world of high fashion.
>
> She has been criticized for her 'cut price' clothes, but in fairness the Princess dressed this way before her marriage, and her late mother-in-law, Princess

Marina, had exactly the same arrangements with
the big couture houses. She has very few clothes,
but they are all carefully chosen to mix and match.

After realizing how tight money was going to be, the
new Princess made the decision to take selected commissions from clients who wanted their houses or offices redecorated. Prince Michael checked with the Queen to find
out if this would be permitted and was told that the
Princess could do as she wished as long as she didn't
use her position to influence prospective clients – though
logically the very fact of her position would be reason
enough for many people to seek her services.

'I think the Princess thought that once you were a
Princess, you asked for what you wanted and you got it.
The world was your oyster,' John Barratt said.

She talked herself into believing that if she put on
a good show, in time she would get on the civil list.
It won't ever happen. They are just not entitled to
money from the State. It's bad luck for them, but
it is the rules. And in some ways it is unjust. They
are not supposed to accept invitations from abroad
without clearing it with the Queen's secretary. The
Princess probably wouldn't bother if she were popping over to Paris to see friends, but technically she
is supposed to get permission. They may not be on
the civil list, but the restrictions still apply.

He says that Princess Michael is a perfectionist, which
makes her appear high-handed on occasions, and that she
can rant and rave, but like all volatile people she can also
be extremely tender and compassionate.

She does wear the trousers and boss him about. But
then he's the sort of person who needs a little boss-
ing. But the endearing thing about the Prince and
Princess is that they are so much in love.
There is no doubt that his affable, easy-going

nature is a foil to her fiery temperament. He appears shy; in private he is extremely funny. I have often seen him melt his wife's anger into tears of laughter. One thing is certain. The Prince could not be more proud of his wife.

'It's a pity Lord Mountbatten didn't live longer,' he added. 'He'd have been the one to knock her into shape. Harnessed in the right direction, she could be an asset to the family. But someone has to keep her under control.'

John Barratt had been Lord Mountbatten's private secretary, and after he was murdered by the IRA in 1979 Princess Michael approached him and asked if he would be interested in working for them. Sir Peter Scott, who had seen them through their marriage, was leaving.

After a hiccup or two about the salary, which was not all he had expected, John Barratt agreed to take the job. He was not entirely certain it was a good idea. Prince Charles, who had known Barratt for all the years he looked after Mountbatten, wasn't certain, either.

They met by chance at a concert in Liverpool, and the Prince said: 'I hear you're going to the Kents.'

'I'm going to try, Sir,' Barratt said.

'Are you sure?' the Prince said. 'You know what she's like.'

'Oh, well,' said Barratt, making a joke, 'she can't be worse than Uncle Dickie!'

What did really upset the Prince was when Barratt was told that, though he had been Uncle Dickie's private secretary for so many years, because he was now working for the royal family he could not be a private secretary, only a common-or-garden ordinary one. The reason? He had never held a commission when he was in the Royal Navy where Mountbatten had first found him.

Prince Charles wrote Barratt a furious letter from India where he was touring in December 1980, saying that he was appalled that John could not be accepted as private

secretary to Prince Michael. He said he could not understand how such a thing could happen and that when he
got back he was determined to make a nuisance of himself
about it. He said he had never heard anything so ridicu-
lous in his life and would greatly enjoy making a fuss
about it. He also knew exactly what Lord Mountbatten's
reaction would have been.

John Barratt was very touched by the letter, but he
never did become Prince Michael's 'private' secretary.

Mountbatten himself had not been the easiest man to
work for. Barratt said that if they didn't have a row at
least every Friday fortnight something was wrong. After
he left the Princess's employment, he also said that the
difference between the two jobs was that when Lord
Mountbatten was wrong and had behaved badly he knew
how to apologize.

It was through Lord Mountbatten that the Prince and
Princess became friendly with the octagenarian romantic
novelist, Barbara Cartland. Though the Princess is a
favourite of Miss Cartland, she does not rate so highly
with her staff. One weekend when she and the Prince
were house-guests, she came down about ten to find the
house deserted.

'Where is everyone?' she demanded of a servant.

'The guns went out at half-past nine, your Royal
Highness,' she was told.

'How dare they go without me,' exploded the Princess.
'Don't they realize I'm royal!'

It was that reaction that caused one of Barbara
Cartland's staff to remark: 'Her Royal Highness is very
beautiful, but she has no class.'

It is her tactlessness and the way she speaks without
thinking that does cause many of Princess Michael's problems; yet, rather more endearingly, she can be astonish-
ingly unguarded and open.

She put her size-seven foot right in it when she made

a couple of most unfortunate remarks to two actors at a charity gala. It was at the National Theatre production of *Guys and Dolls*, and backstage she met Norman Rossington, who is perhaps not the tallest actor in the business. She asked him if his name was Lofty. She was then introduced to American actor, Clarke Peters, and cheerfully said that she presumed he was known as Chalky. Mr Peters is black, and found this remark grossly impertinent and offensive. And an exchange of letters began with Buckingham Palace which ended with the Queen's Deputy Private Secretary stating that Princess Michael admitted the remark and immediately regretted it. She upset her nearest neighbours at Kensington Palace, Prince Charles and Princess Diana, by another piece of tactlessness. Prince Charles's butler, Alan Fisher, had said a very rude word in her son Lord Frederick's hearing. Lord Frederick had repeated it, and she tore the butler off a strip. She promptly received a curt note from Prince Charles tearing her off a strip, saying that if his staff needed telling off he'd do it himself, thank you very much.

The *Mirror*'s James Whitaker tells of another occasion when she upset Prince Charles. A man from the Department of the Environment was showing the Prince around Kensington Palace before he and Princess Diana moved in. She pushed her way in on the tour, and then monopolized the official's time complaining about a drain in her apartments.

But, then, the royal family can be very tetchy with her. When she asked for advice about what she should wear to a state funeral she received a one-word note in reply: 'Black.' After the funeral, she received an even tetchier note. 'When I say black, I mean black. Not a black handbag with gold clasps.'

She is often let down by her friends. She introduced Princess Diana to David and Elizabeth Emanuel, who made the Princess of Wales's wedding dress. Unfortunately, the Waleses and the Emanuels fell out when the Prince and Princess felt, wrongly or rightly, that the Emanuels were cashing in on their name.

Ingrid Seward, the editor of *Majesty*, is one of the few journalists who have been granted an interview at the Princess's Kensington Palace apartment. Ingrid decided to request an interview after she received several letters from the Princess's secretary asking for copies of photographs that the magazine had printed. To Ingrid's delight and surprise, the request was granted.

It just happened to be pouring with rain on the day when, accompanied by writer Christopher Warwick, she plodded up the road to Kensington Palace getting wetter and wetter. Being a girl from an upper-class county family herself she naturally made for Princess Michael's front door.

> We were told very sternly by the butler that we should have gone to the tradesmen's entrance. But he did let us in and helped us dry off a bit. Then we waited in this beautiful drawing-room – all blue and grey watered silk walls. When she came in she immediately removed some drooping roses and gave them to her lady-in-waiting to take away. 'Have you ever seen such sad flowers,' she said.
>
> I must say I found her perfectly charming and very easy to talk to. Well, actually she herself is very happy to talk. She emphasizes words a great deal and waves her hands about a lot in a very Continental way. She also has this rather odd accent which is hard to place. It's certainly not Australian. It sounds German, but why should she have a German accent? She has the most beautiful skin and that marvellous tangly hair.
>
> The writer and I had great difficulty not laughing when she said: 'I love your magazine. My Nanny took it. That's how I saw it first.' She added that normally she only ever reads *The Times*.
>
> We found her very open and not averse to getting

the odd little dig in about 'the family' as she called them. She gave the impression that they only communicate with each other through notes or memos. But what I found astonishing were some of the stories she told against herself. She knew she was speaking to two journalists and there was a tape-recorder going, but it didn't seem to trouble her.

She told how she was woken up one morning by a noise outside her bedroom. She went to the window in her négligé and peeped through. There seemed to be some sort of disturbance going on downstairs, so she rang the policeman at the gates to see what was happening.

It was a group of children singing 'Happy Birthday' to Princess Diana, whose birthday it was. Princess Michael must have complained, because she told us how Prince Charles and Princess Diana had said: 'You're not really going to make a fuss about a few little girls singing "Happy Birthday".'

Majesty did not print the story. They did print her grumbles about money. How much postage cost, how much secretarial help cost, and how Princess Michael said of her husband: 'I do believe that his image is that of a hard-working member of his family, albeit one without a civil list allocation, which can probably never be changed. The rules were made a long time ago.'

'Probably never be changed'? It does sound as if she had still not quite given up hope. Yet on another occasion she proclaimed passionately that 'We don't want to be on the civil list or we should totally lose our independence' – regardless of the fact that they could have their independence any time they wanted.

Ingrid Seward said that she and Christopher Warwick left 'loving' the Princess. 'We honestly thought she was terrific. She has such charm, and she is fascinating. The only Achilles heel we could see was a preoccupation with money. She seemed to think and talk about money a lot. But, then, it did sound as if they were short of it.'

Stephen Barry, Prince Charles's ex-valet, has written two books that have never been published in Britain. He gives a revealing, below-stairs view of the Princess, pointing out that she has the sort of smart taste that the royals with their love for anything cosy automatically distrust.

In his book *Royal Secrets* he tells how the Princess managed to irritate the Queen the first time that she and Prince Michael were invited to Windsor for Christmas. The Queen put them in the Edward III Tower, which has the most modern interior, having been completely redecorated in the sixties. Princess Michael took one look round and said to the page who was showing her the suite: 'This décor is awful.' The page trotted back and told the Queen, who was not amused. It now looks as if the Queen's little joke will be never to house Princess Michael anywhere else than in the Edward III Tower.

Stephen Barry also tells how there was a great deal of hilarity below stairs about Princess Michael's roof garden. The Department of the Environment had built a superb roof terrace for Prince Charles's apartment at Kensington Palace. It is large, sunny, and runs the full length of two apartments. It has a greenhouse, a barbecue and garden furniture. And it is not overlooked.

Watching this transformation of the roof, Princess Michael wanted one, too. Her request was turned down flat as being too costly, and also structurally impossible. Not to be defeated, she asked Michael Heseltine, the Secretary for the Environment of the time, to dinner. Towards the end of the meal she tackled him on the subject. Her ploy was: 'Wouldn't it be lovely for the children to have some fresh air in London?' Somewhat trapped, Michael Heseltine agreed that it would be lovely and, yes, she could have a terrace. She neglected to mention the small garden that goes with the apartment and, happily for her, he did not know of its existence.

Her terrace was built, but it doesn't quite match up to the Waleses'. Hers clings to the side of the building with room for just two chairs on artificial grass. It's not exactly private, being overlooked by both the Waleses and their staff, if they take the trouble to hang out of the window.

Staff don't stay long with the Princess. One of Prince Charles's valets went as her butler, but said he couldn't stand the pretension. One of his duties was to drive her car and act as chauffeur. It was not a royal-type sedan car, but a green Jaguar. Once, when he was driving her to the Victoria and Albert Museum, she suddenly demanded that he put on all the inside lights: 'So people can see me.'

'It wasn't that sort of car,' the butler said. 'It would have looked silly arriving in a Jag with the inside lights on. I just got out and let her out as quickly as possible.'

His replacement butler didn't stay long, either. One weekend at the house in the country, she asked him if he was interested in painting. When he said yes, thinking she meant oils or watercolours, she briskly said in that case he could paint the stables. White.

But it is the *folie de grandeur* which makes her most unpopular. Rank is important to her. For a long time she had her secretary send her engagements to *The Times* court circular page. *The Times* would publish her engagements, but under a line, ruling them off from the day's main events. She guards her place in the royal pecking order diligently. And even her closest friends don't escape from her obsession with the order of precedence.

The Prince and Princess were invited by her great friend, Princess Esra of Hyderabad, to a dinner at her home. The Spanish ambassador and his wife were to be present. On the morning of the dinner, the Princess telephoned Princess Esra to discuss who outranked whom.

Princess Esra, who is the daughter of the last Sultan of Turkey, wasn't very interested, and sidestepped the issue.

Later in the morning, Princess Esra's secretary received a call from Princess Michael's office, demanding that the matter be sorted out. The secretary phoned the Foreign Office and was told that the Spanish ambassador, being a representative of the King of Spain, certainly took precedence over a minor English prince and his wife.

A similar incident took place when the Princess was making a private visit to Marbella in 1984 as the guest of Wafik Said, a Middle Eastern oil millionaire. She was to attend a Red Cross ball, held at the Rodeo Club. The Foreign Office were said to have advised against the trip, but she was set on going. Before leaving, she told her lady-in-waiting, Anne Frost, to telephone the office of Lavinia, Duchess of Norfolk to say that Princess Michael wished to be officially received when she arrived at Gatwick airport in Sussex, her point of departure for Spain, so that Lavinia, as the Lord Lieutenant of the County, could see that proper arrangements were made. Lavinia Norfolk declined the request when she discovered that the Princess's visit to Spain was a private one, and therefore not officially requiring a reception committee.

Furious, Princess Michael telephoned her sister-in-law, Princess Alexandra, asking her to intervene and use her influence on Lavinia Norfolk's daughter, Lady Mary Fitzalan Howard. Lady Mary is Princess Alexandra's childhood friend, and also her lady-in-waiting. Marie-Christine wanted Alexandra to persuade her to persuade her mother to reverse the decision. Lady Mary declined to call her mother on the matter.

She alienated another old friend when she was showing off her Kensington Palace drawing-room. One by one she showed her friend some of the treasures, including a collection of Fabergé that Prince Michael had inherited from his mother. The house is full of beautiful things, many of them from the Buckingham Palace store-rooms, which were opened to her when she was ready to furnish her apartments.

The Thai maid was serving afternoon tea when her friend said: 'MC, you are lucky, and all your friends are so happy for you.'

When the maid had left, the Princess snapped: 'Don't you ever call me MC in front of the servants again!'

It has also been reported that she once enraged the Queen by inferring that Michael of Kent was more royal than the monarch and other members of her family. The Queen is said to have taken the remark as a slight on her own mother, Queen Elizabeth, the Queen Mother, who was born Lady Elizabeth Bowes Lyon and, though of noble lineage, not royal.

It seems an incredibly tactless thing to have said to the Queen, even from one as tactless as Princess Michael. The probable truth is that she said it to someone else, and word got back, as word always does, to the royal family.

In a way, she was quite correct. Prince Michael's father, Edward of Kent, was the only child of King George V and Queen Mary to marry a royal – Princess Marina of Greece. His brother, Edward VIII, abdicated when he married his American divorcee; brother Bertie, George VI, married Lady Elizabeth Bowes Lyon; Harry of Gloucester married a Scottish noblewoman, Lady Alice Montagu Douglas Scott; and the Princess Royal married a Yorkshire landowner, Henry Lascelles, 6th Earl of Harewood.

So the Princess's remark that Michael is very royal is quite true. In royal terms he is as pure as it is possible to be. His paternal grandparents were George V and Queen Mary, and Queen Mary had been a Princess of Teck. His maternal great-grandparents were George I of Greece and the Grand Duchess Olga of Russia, and his mother's parents were Prince and Princess Nicholas of Greece. Prince Nicholas died in 1938. Princess Nicholas, who was an aunt by marriage of the Duke of Edinburgh, had been born a Russian Imperial Grand Duchess and cousin of the last Tsar of Russia. She died in 1957.

She was most upset, too, when she found out that her son and daughter would not be a little prince and princess. It had to be explained to her that English royal titles die out after two generations. George V, that wiliest of monarchs, decreed he would not have his kingdom become a second Ruritania, plastered with princes and princesses. Only the children and grandchildren of the sovereign were to be royal.

Princess Michael's children, as offspring of the younger son of a royal duke, are allowed the style of younger children of an ordinary duke. Her first boy would be a lord, and her daughter lady. Her down-to-earth mother, Countess Rogala-Koczorowski, was less concerned with titles. When she first saw her grandson after his birth and noted that he had huge hands, she said she hoped he would become a plumber. 'A plumber's life pays well,' she said.

Princess Michael became pregnant immediately after the marriage. She said: 'Even the rose named after me, the Princess Michael of Kent, is down in the catalogue as a good propagator.' But it is unlikely that her children will ever be required for royal duties. By the time they are teenagers, Prince Charles's children will be old enough to undertake engagements. And no doubt Prince Charles and Princess Diana will wish they could spare them from this life of duty. Certainly Princess Anne has made it clear that she will be very content if her children are never involved and are allowed to live private lives. Princess Alexandra's attitude to her children's anonymity is so strong that her husband, Angus Ogilvy, refused to accept a peerage because it would have made his children titled.

The royal family, all of whom would rather be private citizens, find it very odd that Princess Michael, who need have absolutely nothing to do with the royal round, is so keen to be part of it. Princess Margaret is forever telling her children that they are not royal just because their aunt happens to be the Queen. But if members of the family put themselves in the public eye they are supposed to keep up the standards.

In the summer of 1985 the Queen personally sent Princess Michael a number of memos after she had done things that the monarch felt were not in keeping with being royal.

One arrived on Princess Michael's desk after she had had a night out at Annabel's nightclub in Berkeley Square in the heart of London's Mayfair. An onlooker at the next table to the Princess's party spoke to one of the Palace secretaries about the Princess's behaviour that night, and the result was a 'don't do it' note from the Queen.

Many of Princess Michael's troubles have been caused by her complete inability to keep a low profile. She loves her own prominence, but worries about how the other royal women react.

'You must understand that I come very low in the pecking order,' she said, lowering her hand to near the ground.

> I am here. I must not be thought to be pushing my way up. I am not royal at all. I am not special for myself but because I married into a great family. And I want everyone who meets me to enjoy it and have a good time. The tickets for the charity functions I attend cost a bomb, so of course people expect me to be nice and sing for my supper.

All very true. But it's difficult to control a naturally extrovert nature – together with being smart, which the royal family are not, and being clever, which the royal family are but not in the same way. Marie-Christine, they believe, is 'clever-clever', and this has led to her unpopularity with the family. Sometimes they are unfairly irritated by her. The royals are doggie people – the Queen with her eleven corgis, the Queen Mother with two, and Prince Charles with his Labrador. Unfortunately, Princess Michael likes cats and owns a fleet of Siamese. The royal family can't stand cats. They don't own one between them.

The sad thing is that Mountbatten was right. Handled properly Princess Michael could have been an asset to the family. Her instinct in public situations can be superb. She has the ability to make people warm to her. The Chief Nursing Officer at the Great Ormond Street Hospital for Sick Children, Miss Betty Barchard, describes her as an 'absolute sweety'. The Princess had presented the student nurses' awards, and Miss Barchard said: 'She's so natural and unaffected and she works so hard. The nurses and their parents absolutely loved her.'

She herself said that she would not have made so many mistakes if she had had a mother-in-law to guide her. She had won the battle when she married the Prince. If she had been able to keep a low profile, she might just have won the war. 'Admittedly, we didn't realize we would be so public,' the Princess explained. 'My husband never had been, so we didn't think that anyone would find us at all interesting. We thought we'd be able to slip in under the woodwork.'

It is remarks like that which, coming from a woman who could, if she wished, have led a totally private life, make the royals very cross indeed.

As a family of horse-lovers, they should have applauded when Princess Michael began to hunt with the Beaufort and the Cotswolds. She also took up dressage at the age of thirty-nine after her second child was born. And she didn't take half-measures. She engaged the top English equestrienne, Pammy Siveright, to teach her and she took private lessons in competitive riding at the Talland School of Equitation near her Gloucestershire home. It took courage to attempt something so specialized so late in life. Many people, though, regarded it as another example of her 'anything you can do I can do better' mentality. It was thought that she was going to try to outdo Princess Anne. 'Not true,' she said. 'In the family we have people who really know what they are doing in a serious way. I've taken it [riding] up because we are in the country and I'm lucky having two horses.'

There was no competition between the two royal riders. As it happened, Princess Anne, at the age of thirty-four, had decided to give up competitive riding just about the time Princess Michael was ready to begin.

Princess Michael says her nerves are at breaking-point when she is in the ring. 'It's not because I'm Princess Michael, it's because I'm me! I get those awful mental blanks. It's sheer performance nerves. I'm less nervous making a speech in front of a thousand people. My mother was an Olympic skier, but I've never competed in sport before and I'm frightened.'

She acquitted herself well in the ring, but once again she went over the top. She began taking lessons in riding side-saddle. The only woman in the royal family who rides in that fashion is the Queen. And the only time she does so is when she is conducting the Trooping the Colour ceremony.

By the time her fortieth birthday arrived on 15 January 1985, Princess Michael had given up trying to please the royal family. She was flying backwards and forwards to America, to Paris, anywhere she felt like going, without reference to Buckingham Palace and frequently without her husband. While playing the Princess, she was also leading a secret and alarming private life. Almost as if to fan the flames she had a fortieth-birthday portrait released of herself, all bare shoulders and flowing hair, which was definitely more Hollywood than Windsor. It was a 'look at me' picture, stating defiantly to the royal family: 'I'm more glamorous and interesting than the rest of you put together.' Which, though it may be truth, did little to increase her popularity.

She gave interviews and, leaving the children at home, she and Michael went off to open Peter de Savary's St James's Club in Antigua when it was reported that he had given them a piece of land worth £150,000. This he denies: 'They like Antigua and are going to build a little house there where they can holiday with their kids. We were able to organize the financing in such a way that they will rent it out and it will pay for itself.'

In Great Britain it was the coldest winter for years, and a magazine ran a feature article on the couple which read: 'Leaving behind arctic conditions in Britain, Prince and Princess Michael of Kent flew to the tranquil Caribbean island of Antigua.' This was the type of publicity which causes the Duke of Edinburgh to explode and remark that monarchies have crumbled for less.

With the club safely declared open, Prince and Princess flew to Barbados to stay with their friend, the insurance magnate, Ronnie Driver. While England froze, the monarch's cousin and his wife were pictured in full colour wind sailing, horse-riding and being welcomed to the tropical paradise by perspiring members of a local band in full dress uniform. The Princess looked stunning in a white cotton dress, sandals and a straw hat. Her besotted husband, trailing along with her, wore shorts and a T-shirt.

The Princess was out of control. And then in April something happened that should have brought her to her senses.

Chapter 5

The Past Returns

APRIL 15th, 1985 was not one of the better days in Princess Michael's life. It was downhill all the way after she received a telephone call from Michael Shea, the former diplomat turned mystery-writer who is press secretary to the Queen.

The *Mirror* had just been on the phone to him at Buckingham Palace informing him that they were about to publish details of the Princess's father's involvement with the Nazi Party and the SS. They wanted some comment from the Palace. An alarmed Michael Shea said he knew nothing about any such thing but that he'd ask Princess Michael.

She, too, appeared to Shea to be alarmed by the news. Her first reaction was that she had never heard any such stories, but that she would ask her mother. In any case, she added, she would sue the *Mirror* if they published. She would call Shea back.

It was midnight in Australia, but the matter could not wait. The Princess said she rang her seventy-two-year-old mother and was told that the story was true. It seems there was a heated row on the telephone, with the Princess shouting at her mother and leaving her in tears.

Afterwards there was endless speculation as to whether the Princess did know or did not know. Was her telephone call really necessary? Some schools of thought said she must have been aware, and it seems most likely that she was. But it is fair to say that she was not even born when her father was expelled from the SS and that she was just a few days old when the Nazi Party also expelled him. Yet, in view of the year she spent in Mozambique with him as a sixteen-year-old, could she really have been ignorant of the truth?

Her mother, however, backs up her daughter's plea of ignorance. A woman of considerable dignity, she said that she regretted she had kept her husband's Nazi past secret from her daughter. As she explained: 'I hadn't been on very good terms with my first husband, and I said to myself: "Why should I say anything?" I regret it now in hindsight very much. I should have been honest. I should have told her. You see, I didn't think it would matter so much. It wouldn't have served much purpose. Now, of course, I'm terribly sorry.'

Whether the Princess knew or did not know would have changed nothing. The *Mirror* were going to publish and be damned. There was nothing to hold them back. They had a photocopy of von Reibnitz's letters to the SS Race Purity Office purporting to prove that he had no Jewish blood in him. It was signed with a Heil Hitler salutation. There was a copy of another document which gave the Princess's father the right to wear the death's-head badge on his SS uniform, and there was also his application to the SS for permission to marry the Princess's mother.

And the *Mirror* had this information all to themselves.

The story had walked into their offices in the shape of black-bearded Dr Philip Hall, a part-time college lecturer at a not very prestigious college in Paddington, west London. In his early thirties, he was engaged in writing an attack on the royal family. The *Mirror* did not name this source when they went to town with his story on the morning of the sixteenth. Perhaps because Hall was a left-wing socialist, a former official of the Trotskyist International Socialist Party and active in the extreme Socialist Workers' Party. He had also been investigated – frequently – by Special Branch.

Hall insisted he had stumbled across his story 'purely by chance' while engaged in routine research on backgrounds of the royal family. One wonders where he can have been looking. He also admitted he wanted to see the monarchy abolished. 'I would describe myself as a Republican,' he said to a *News of the World* reporter when his identity was out in the open, 'and Republicans would like to see a Republic, not a Monarchy. I thought the story was being covered up, so I decided to do something.'

His reasons were not entirely altruistic. He took his information first to *Stern*, Germany's largest magazine. He asked for £15,000. They turned him down. He then peddled his wares to the *Mirror*, who paid him somewhat less: £1000.

It was bad luck for Princess Michael that his 'stumblings' were to affect her so seriously. She had already had enough problems with popularity. The public had taken to her, but the royal family remained cool, if not icy. She knew the minute Michael Shea called that something had to be done. Quickly.

She began by ringing her husband telling him to come

117

home. He came immediately to Kensington Palace and discussed what was to be done. But until they knew whether or not the *Mirror* would run the story there was not a great deal that could be done. The Princess spent a lot of time on the telephone that day, ringing her various relatives around the world and checking on facts that she said her mother had given her.

The *Mirror*'s front page on 16 April read: 'PRINCESS MICHAEL'S FATHER IN GERMAN SS.'

> Buckingham Palace confirmed to the *Mirror* last night that the father of Princess Michael was a member of the Nazi German SS. Michael Shea, Press Secretary to the Queen, said: 'Princess Michael confirmed tonight that it is true that her father was a member of the SS.
>
> 'It came as a total surprise to her when she heard the news from James Whitaker [a *Mirror* reporter].
>
> 'And it came as a total shock.
>
> 'There will be no more comment or statement from the Princess.'

Inside the paper a headline in tombstone type blared: 'PROOF OF SS MEMBERSHIP.' It went on to read:

> Princess Michael of Kent's aristocratic father, Baron von Reibnitz was a leading member of Hitler's dreaded SS. His SS number was 060 010. And on his black uniform he wore a death's head badge.
>
> A personal friend of Goering, who recommended at least one of his postings, von Reibnitz took this terrible secret to the grave when he died, two years ago in Germany.

Good stirring stuff. The *Mirror* had been doing some of its homework thoroughly. They had tracked down Princess Michael's half-sister, who 'talked about the 11 years their father would never discuss'.

'Shattered by the news,' said the *Mirror*,

Magrit Francisco of Illinois said: 'I knew he was a member of the Nazi party but I did not know he was in the SS.

'It is very hurtful to learn this. The Gestapo and the SS did terrible things in the war.

'All of us who grew up in that atmosphere of Germany at that time will have to bear the results as a cross until the day we die.

'But knowing my father and the gentle person he was, I cannot believe that he could personally do anything dreadful to anybody.'

The *Mirror* went on to say:

The news that Baron von Reibnitz was in the SS explains why he has always been a mystery figure in Princess Michael's life.

He was not at Princess Michael's wedding in Vienna in 1978 and there was never any discussion about him.

Unfortunately for the *Mirror*, he was very much at the wedding, aged eighty-one, still with hair, a moustache and charm, looking like everyone's favourite grandpa. It was an error the paper had to reverse, when without a blush of shame they splashed the wedding picture on the front page the following day, showing the Baron standing between Angus Ogilvy and Princess Anne.

Back home at Kensington Palace it was Michael Shea's statement from Buckingham Palace that there would be no further comment or statement from the Princess that was most troubling Marie-Christine. She was growing uneasy about claims that she had been aware of her father's past. And it was at that fortuitous moment that Timothy Aitken telephoned and asked if he could come and see her immediately. Aitken is a business associate of Prince Michael and chief executive of TV-am.

In the Princess's drawing-room at Kensington Palace,

Aitken said that she must end the rumours before the situation was out of hand. He pointed out that she would get not a moment's peace from the press until she made some statement herself. What he was suggesting was that she should give an interview on TV-am; that she should let a television crew into her apartment and pre-record the programme. If she liked it, it would be screened; if she didn't, there was no harm done.

The Princess agonized, but gradually warmed to the idea. She called in Colonel Michael Farmer, the private secretary she shares with her husband, to tell him what she had decided to do. He was appalled at the suggestion, knowing that Buckingham Palace would never agree. Royalty ride storms without comment. He consulted with Michael Shea, who was equally horrified, and came back to put the royal viewpoint firmly and clearly to the Princess. The interview must not take place.

There was instant pressure from royal advisers to stop the programme going ahead. It was inferred that the Queen did not agree, but the Princess refused to listen. She had made up her mind and she was determined to do the interview. She pointed out that she had the power of veto if anything went wrong. She felt safe with TV-am's promise of retraction. Aitken is a personal friend, and her husband was on the board of Aitken Hume, the finance company part-owned by Aitken.

The television cameras arrived. Just as they were setting up their equipment, Prince Michael came home from his day in the City. He was not pleased to find his drawing-room taken over by television cameras, but Timothy Aitken persuaded him to let the interview go ahead and make the final decision later. The Prince, under the circumstances, had little choice but to agree. The Princess then made one request. She asked if he would leave the room while the interview took place. His presence, she said, would make her nervous.

It was all over by six o'clock, and the Prince and Princess with Aitken sat down to watch the BBC news. They were aware that the story of the Princess's father must be the lead item, but they were not prepared for the old newsreel footage of cattle-trucks filled with people on their way to concentration-camps. The implications were clear. Von Reibnitz had sent people to their death.

Princess Michael decided then that her side of the story must be made public. She told Aitken that she wanted to go ahead with the interview.

Later that evening Colonel Farmer with the Prince and Timothy Aitken watched a video of the Princess's interview, and it became clear that she was extremely convincing in her handling of the carefully chosen questions. Even Colonel Farmer had to agree that she had done remarkably well. But he repeated his warnings that the programme should not be screened.

In the end, it was Prince Michael who gave the go-ahead. Timothy Aitken then went back to TV-am's studios, happy with his scoop.

Just after he left, Lady Elizabeth Anson, a great-niece of the Queen Mother and caterer extraordinaire to the royal family, came by. She had catered for not just one but both of Marie-Christine's weddings, and she was delivering a birthday present for Lady Gabriella Windsor, her god-daughter. It had not been her intention to go into the Princess's apartment but, pressed, she did so. She commented later that the air could have been cut with a knife, and neither Prince nor Princess seemed at all happy.

Lady Elizabeth drank a glass of soda water and left.

An hour later the Kents with the rest of the royal family were on their way to Windsor for a state banquet in honour of President Hastings Banda of Malawi. The Princess looked her usual stunning self.

The news was abroad of what she had done; ITV had been screening trailers for the morning's broadcast, and they had not escaped the royal family's attention. The Princess came under more pressure to cancel the interview. She continued to refuse.

The next morning at 6.35 a.m. Princess Michael appeared on the nation's television screens, looking pale and distressed, the Palace dictum that there would be no more comment or statement ignored. It was one of the most dramatic interviews ever given by a member of the royal family, and the Princess gave the performance of her life. Wearing a long white dress and with her long blonde hair loose over her shoulders, she was interviewed by Nick Owen, who led her through the interview with sympathy and a lot of hushed tones on both sides. Aitken had chosen him for the job because he had met the Princess on a couple of occasions at Aitken's home. Cool, relaxed and confident, the Princess grabbed the public's sympathy with her seeming openness and honesty. Her instincts to face the foe, like her father before her, had been accurate. Palace advisers had been wrong.

Nick Owen's first question was whether she knew of her father's involvement in the SS. Holding her hands in a gesture of appeal, she said:

> He did join the SS. I had no idea. I think it was sufficiently shocking to me that he had been in the Nazi Party but I didn't think to look further had there been more than that, had it been worse than that, and I think it came as a very great blow to me because I always sort of hero-worshipped him.

Owen suggested that there was a school of thought that believed she knew the truth but had just kept quiet.

'Well,' said the Princess,

> I don't consider myself such a stupid person, to be frank with you, because things like that always come out and for me to live trembling, fearing such a knowledge would come out would be very stupid.

Also I would then have at my disposal for immediate transmission to the Press and to yourself, the document which actually exonerates him, which states clearly that his position in the SS was an honorary position.

He never served for the SS. He never wore the uniform, to which, it is true, he was entitled, and so that in fact, if I had known, I would have this exonerating information to hand.

As it was, I immediately telephoned my mother when I was told that this report was coming out in the *Mirror* yesterday and said more or less to the effect: 'Guess what they are trying to pin on me now?'; and she said: 'But I am afraid it is true.' And so I said: 'Well, how is that possible?', and so she told me what I have told you.

It was a total shock to everything I have been taught to believe, you know, but my shoulders are broad and I shall have to carry it.

I was desperately ashamed at first and then when I spoke to my brother and he explained to me the document which exonerated my father from any activity which I have been brought up to believe, you know, that the SS meant one thing, basically concentration-camps for Jews and so on.

I have now discovered that he was not involved with anything like that at all, so I am relieved to discover that. But, yes, it is a deep shame for me ... none the less it is a dreadful thing and I shall have to live with it.

Her answers to questions gave the impression that she believed the royal family might have known: 'I presume that one was investigated; I always took it for granted I was investigated, so I don't know.'

She told the nation that she had had messages of support from the royal family and her husband was also supportive and as devastated as she was.

'It is like suddenly discovering you are adopted, you know,' she said.

> Here I am forty years old and I suddenly discover something that is really quite unpleasant and I shall simply have to live with it.
>
> What the public's perception of me will be I don't know. I wasn't alive when all this happened, so I hope they will judge me on my own perform-ance and what I am and what I stand for.

Meanwhile the *Mirror* were hanging on to their story like a dog with a bone. 'THIS BLOODY DISGRACE,' they trumpeted all over the front page, with a three-inch swastika to make the point.

While Princess Michael was wooing the viewers, the *Mirror* was telling its readers:

> The statement by Buckingham Palace last night that Princess Michael never knew her father was a major in the SS is unbelievable. . . .
>
> How could it be possible that 40 years should pass without the Princess not knowing [sic] her father was a prominent Nazi and SS officer?
>
> . . . The Princess said last night that the news had come as a shock to her.
>
> Does it mean it was also a shock to her husband? To the Queen? To the senior Palace officials?
>
> If they didn't know it, why didn't they? If they did – which seems much more likely – who con-cealed it?
>
> The Princess says that she will not be making any further statement. She will find she will have to.
>
> The Royal family is Britain's prize possession. Even 40 years on, the taint of Nazism undermines it.

By now the Princess, ever quick off the mark, had al-ready made her statement. And, in doing so, had deflected much of the criticism against herself. Nor was she too displeased at the BBC's pirating of the interview – a move that Timothy Aitken said would 'cost the BBC zillions'. From the Kents' point of view, the more viewers the merrier.

Colonel Farmer, lamely explaining why the Princess chose to appear on television, said:

> The Princess felt, like many people, that there was so much speculation going on that she really ought to say something.
>
> This just happens to be an approach that appealed to her.

The *Sun*, realizing which way the wind was blowing, conducted a poll, and came out with a front page declaring: 'WE STILL LOVE YOU, PRINCESS MICHAEL.' It seemed that 95 per cent of Britain supported the Princess. 'The nation's heart goes out to you,' it assured her.

In Double Bay, Sydney, where Princess Michael's mother, the Countess Rogala-Koczorowski, lives, the media set up camp. She was not commenting, but the Princess's half-brother, Mathias, said he knew nothing about his mother's ex-husband's activities. He said that a statement would be made later. With that he flashed a knowing smile and vanished inside. The statement was never made.

Ten days later Princess Michael won more public sympathy when speaking at a Doctor of the Year lunch, organized by BUPA, the private health insurers.

After handing over a cheque for £1000 she stood wearing a plain black suit and a white blouse to address the 450 doctors and their guests. 'It has not been an easy ten days,' she said, and a ripple of laughter ran around the Savoy Hotel banqueting-room. But it rapidly became clear that this was not the Princess's little joke. 'You must understand,' she went on. 'It's been a very difficult time for me.' And as she struggled to control tears the laughter turned to sympathetic applause.

'I would like to take this opportunity', she persisted, 'to thank the thousands of people who have written to me.' She was by now in tears, and paused for composure. Then she added: 'And just to say that I will answer everyone in time.'

She was rewarded with enthusiastic applause and a standing ovation.

The press, too, were now solidly on her side, thundering on a 'sins of the father' tack. Her Majesty the Queen, however, was enraged yet again. Royalty are not supposed to cry in public. Not even at the funerals of those they love. It was another black mark for Princess Michael.

It took some days for the story to go away completely. There was desperate thrashing around in the press to pin something positive on the Baron. The difficulty was that his Gestapo file, hastily brought from Berlin, seemed, as the Princess had said, to exonerate him. The popular papers fell upon the fact that, in belonging to the SS, von Reibnitz would have been a member of the Lebensborn ('Source of Life') programme with which Hitler planned to produce a blond, blue-eyed master race.

Tall, blonde 'Aryan' girls, usually members of Hitler's girl guide corps, were mated with the élite of SS soldiers in 'stud farms'. The women had to sign a document relinquishing all claims to the babies, future perfect members of Hitler's Third Reich, who were born in twelve Lebensborn homes.

On von Reibnitz's documents the sign, resembling a matchstick in shape, showed that he was a Lebensborn member. But Nana Wiessler, the librarian of the Weiner Library in Devonshire Street, London, where copies of von Reibnitz's documents are held, said: 'This doesn't necessarily mean von Reibnitz was personally involved in the stud farm process. They tended to be men with perfect

Aryan looks.' Also he was considerably older than the fathers who were usually chosen by the SS.

Nazi-hunter Simon Wiesenthal, who is head of the Jewish Documentation Centre in Vienna, also came on to the scene. He confirmed that records showed von Reibnitz was in the Lebensborn programme. 'They also indicate he paid contributions to the scheme, like 99 per cent of SS members. But there is no evidence to indicate his exact role in Lebensborn.'

Eventually the full text of the de-nazification court's ruling on Princess Michael's father was released. Once again braving the lion in its den he himself had appealed to be exonerated. In 1947 an Allied occupation de-nazification court had classified him as a 'Mitlaufer' – a word literally meaning to 'run with'. This was the fourth of five categories of Nazi involvement, running down from the first, who were major offenders and included all top-ranking Nazis. By the time Marie-Christine was three years old and living with her mother in Vienna, the Upper Bavarian Appeal Tribunal gave their decision on 14 May 1948. The text of the Tribunal read:

> The accused joined the party in 1931 [sic] in the belief that National Socialism would bring about economic recovery. Moreover he continued to be politically inactive and accepted no party office.
>
> As a horse-breeder and devotee of equestrian sport, the accused became a member of the Cavalry-SS in 1933.
>
> The accused had been an active hunter from early childhood. He was appointed Chief Ranger and in 1934 became Regional Chief Ranger.

The text went on to say that von Reibnitz had never served in the SS under any rank; had no authority to give orders of any kind; and merely had the right to wear the uniform and hold the rank of captain. It was thus a matter of purely honorary rank.

Perhaps the most important two paragraphs from his daughter's point of view were those that read:

> He never made any secret of his desire to stand apart from the party. As early as 1940 he expressed the views that one could only hope Germany would lose the war since that was the only way in which the Nazi domination could be broken.
>
> The accused concerned himself to the greatest possible extent with the well-being of foreign workers. He went well beyond the limits in helping those subjected to racial persecution.

They did not totally exonerate him. The petition for exoneration could not be allowed, but they ruled him to be a 'less incriminated person'. 'The accused', the report said somewhat contortedly, 'is equivalent to a non-accused person.'

The exoneration cost the Baron fifty Deutschmarks.

Princess Michael was in the clear.

But did the royal family know all the time?

They did. The facts had been made known to them eight months before Marie-Christine became Princess Michael. Harold Brooks-Baker, then of Debrett, had researched the von Reibnitz past at the request of Lord Airley and Lord Rupert Neville, a close friend of the Queen. Lord Rupert died in 1982. The research was not difficult. The papers were there for anyone to find. Philip Hall found them.

The royal family would have been in some difficulty if they had attempted to end Prince Michael's wedding on the grounds of her father's wartime career. The Palace were more concerned with the problems of her first marriage and her Catholicism than with her background. They shared her skeletons in the cupboard when it came to Nazi relations.

The 'German relations' as they are known in the royal family are rarely heard about, though Prince Philip makes a yearly visit to them, and they come to Windsor for a few days every year. When the Queen married in 1947, memories of the war were still fresh. The German relations were not invited.

Prince Christoper August of Hesse, Prince Philip's brother-in-law, who married Philip's favourite sister, Sophie of Greece, was a member of the SS. He died in a plane crash in 1943 while travelling to Italy, carrying a message from Hitler to Mussolini. His brother, Prince Phillip of Hesse, was also SS, and had jurisdiction over the Hadamar Asylum where the SS practised euthanasia on its captives. He was later put into a camp himself for telling Hitler he no longer agreed with the philosophy of the Nazi Party.

The story took two weeks to peter out – fanned back into life as it had been by the Princess's public tears. It was a good story while it lasted, though in retrospect the whole thing seems to have been overblown. The Baron doesn't appear as a bad old boy, no better and no worse than many Germans who survived Hitler's Germany.

When the fuss had died down, the Princess's mother told a reporter that her first husband had become disillusioned over Nazism. He was, she said, a kind of royalist and already against the Hitler regime even when she met him.

But there is no gainsaying that he continued to remain a member of the party and the SS for almost fifteen years.

Perhaps he had little choice, and when two years after his death he was making headlines all over the world he could hardly defend himself.

But his daughter defended herself – brilliantly.

It was possibly that triumph over adversity that gave her the idea that she could get away with anything.

Chapter 6

The Princess in Love

PRINCESS MICHAEL, making the point that she and Prince Michael were the hard-up royals, once said she would go anywhere for a hot dinner.

And it was a very hot dinner, one of Mexican tortillas, eaten in Dallas, Texas, that was to end by giving the Princess a bad attack of romantic indigestion eighteen months later. Today she undoubtedly wishes that she had never set foot in Dallas. The events that were put in train there in October 1983 relentlessly had her sliding back down the slippery social slope that she had clawed her way up with so much skill.

The occasion was the visit of their Royal Highnesses Prince and Princess Michael of Kent to Texas. They were there at the invitation of the US Friends of the

English National Opera from 15 to 20 October 1983.

The trip, all found and paid for, included a brief tour of Austin and Houston. It was a particularly lavish visit beginning with a Concorde flight to New York, then a first-class flight on to Houston. There the Kents, along with the Queen's first cousin, Lord Harewood (who was at that time managing director of the opera company), attended a private reception and ball to benefit the English National Opera.

It was one of those interminable guided tours, with no sight left unseen, that leave the participants praying for respite. On the Sunday, 16 October, the royal party took brunch with Mr and Mrs Jenard Gross, two of Austin's élite, and Prince Michael was then whisked off to NASA to view the American space programme. On the Monday they flew to San Antonio for lunch with an ex-governor of Texas, and that evening a private dinner-party was given by Lord and Lady Harewood.

On Tuesday they left for fateful Dallas arriving at Love Field at 6.15 p.m. from Austin. By this time, what with all this singing for her hot supper, the Princess's gracious smile was wearing thin. It had been a long day starting with a 10.00 flight to Austin where they were to take lunch at the United Bank with James Armstrong, the president of the Bank and director of the Friends of the English National Opera. Luncheon was served at the ungodly hour of 11.30 a.m. Afterwards the royal guests were trotted around the LBJ (Lyndon B. Johnson) Museum and Library, and thence proceeded at a breathless pace to Governor White's mansion where they 'retired' for an hour before attending a tea-party, hosted by Mrs White and Mrs Aaron Kruger, yet two more of Austin's élite.

The flight to Dallas took an hour, and once there things began to look up. They were taken to their accommodation at the magnificent Mansion on Turtle Creek. By

American standards this is a tiny hotel with only 143 rooms, but the carpark is jammed with Mercedes and Cadillacs. A suite costs $800 a night and, not surprisingly, only the rich and famous stay there. Victoria Principal of *Dallas* fame held her wedding there, Larry Hagman uses the bar as a meeting-place, and Neil Diamond always books in when he is in town.

It was all very much Princess Michael's cup of tea!

And the best news was that they had the night off. The evening was marked in the programme 'free time' – or it would have been if the Prince and Princess had not been invited to an informal dinner at Raphael's Mexican restaurant, one of the town's more popular, but exclusive, watering-holes. They drank margaritas and ate tortillas, and the evening was hosted by two leading Dallas socialites: millionaire J. Ward Hunt and his wife, Laura. Ward Hunt was in his early forties, a property-developer and the cousin of oil tycoon Nelson Bunker Hunt. He ran the Bedrock Development Corporation in Dallas and was building a billion-dollar project that would eventually house thirty office buildings, hotels, apartments and shopping-space.

The following day, Wednesday, 19 October, the official programme featured three formal events. There was a tea-party given by Mimi Lay, another of the Dallas variety élite; but lunch with the Dallas business community and a dinner benefit at the Mansion on Turtle Creek – which included a presentation of Dallas débutantes – were both hosted by Laura Hunt.

The guests at the dinner paid $250 to dine with the royal couple, and in his after-dinner speech Prince Michael remarked that his two children, Lord Frederick Windsor and Lady Gabriella Windsor, were so keen on *Dallas* that they had called their pet goats Lucy and Donna. This caused uncertain laughter.

Subsequently, in a summary of the best social events of

1983, the *Dallas Times Herald* placed the benefit dinner in the top ten. The newspaper judged it 'intimate, not stuffy, opulent and elaborate'. 'It was', said the social editor, 'as regal as the attending Royalty.'

If Dallas was impressed by the Princess, she in turn was impressed by the millionaire who had been her host. However, she did also appear to be equally taken by Hunt's wife, a dramatically attractive, dark-haired woman with a Spanish look about her.

The official visit ended the next day with the Prince and Princess making their separate ways back to Britain. The Prince left in the morning, the Princess later that afternoon. No reason for the separate journeys was ever given.

They kept in touch with the Hunts, though in fact Laura and Ward's marriage was already beginning to flounder and divorce was on the cards.

Ten months later, in the autumn of 1984, Ward Hunt was a much poorer man. His wife divorced him in August and she left him reeling from the financial blow. A leading member of Dallas society, Mrs Brooke Stellenwerck-Frampton, said: 'Everyone in Dallas knew it was an ugly divorce. Laura has the kids and she took Ward to the cleaner's.'

Rather like Princess Michael, where Ward Hunt was to burn his fingers yet again, the ex-Mrs Hunt likes the good things of life. Again, like Princess Michael, she has an entourage of some of the world's richest and most famous men. She is friendly with Adnan Khashoggi, Philippe Junot, ex-husband of Princess Caroline, Prince Heinrich and the British Prime Minister's son, Mark Thatcher. She also spends enormous amounts of money proving to herself and to Dallas that she is the hostess with the mostest. This is an exceedingly expensive hobby as in Dallas there is a true wealth of competition to top the social tree.

The ending of his marriage shattered Ward Hunt. Mr

Bill Smith, editor of *Texas Business* magazine, said: 'He had to liquidate some of his assets to pay for the divorce. One was the $4,000,000 stake in the huge Riverside development.' This development of a complex of houses, offices and shops was Ward Hunt's dream project. One he had initiated himself and that was planned to take ten years to complete.

To rub salt in the wound, Laura went on a massive spending spree. She bought a red Ferrari and, for her second car, a top-of-the-range BMW. She moved into a large, white-painted colonial-style house in the University Park district of Dallas, and she had it redecorated from top to bottom to suit her own taste.

It is not really surprising that, after the news of the friendship between her ex-husband and Princess Michael broke, Laura Hunt was said to be furious. She was convinced that, had the facts been publicly known earlier, her financial settlement would have been greater.

What caused the divorce is not known. The only clue came from Laura's father, George Bayoud, who is one of Texas's better-known surgeons. Sounding like any puzzled father, he said that when his daughter first met Ward Hunt she was crazy about him, 'but as the years went by she seemed to tire of him. She told me she found him bland and boring.' Then he added: 'He was very lonely without Laura, but if he was making time with the Princess, he sure was keeping quiet about it.'

The divorce papers were sealed, and Ward Hunt, a reticent man, wasn't talking. Nor, curiously, was his wife. There is no doubt that he was totally besotted with this big blonde, physically (if not materialistically) opposite to his dark-haired and dark-eyed wife. It is difficult to say, as the friendship between him and Princess Michael only seems to have become public at the beginning of 1985. It could, of course, be that prior to 1985 Princess Michael was behaving more discreetly than she did later.

Hunt himself was amazingly close-mouthed. A pay-off of the proportions that Laura Hunt received is a classic example of a saying-goodbye-to-matrimony handout, paid on condition that a tight-lipped silence about something or other is maintained. And subsequent events proved that Ward Hunt was not a man to embarrass the Princess.

It was against this stormy background that Hunt, described as 'shy, retiring and sweet' and 'looking like a chubby Robert Redford', accelerated his courtship of Princess Michael.

He came to Britain and got in touch with her in 1984. On this occasion he was chaperoned by his mother, Jeanne Ward, and they were Princess Michael's guests for lunch at Kensington Palace. His mother said afterwards that the Princess was a perfectly charming hostess. Had the friendship not been innocent at that time, it was bold to visit the lady in her husband's home. But, then, people in love always long to see where and how the loved one lives so they can picture their beloved in their own surroundings. And the fact that Mother came, too, made it perfectly respectable for Hunt to be entertained by the Princess without her husband being present. Whether Mother knew the score is uncertain. Mother confused events later when, besieged by reporters, she said her son was not in love with the Princess, adding: 'At least, I don't think he is.'

The first positive sighting of Ward Hunt and the Princess alone together was in January 1985. Prince and Princess Michael had spent most of January in Antigua with their mutual friend, Peter de Savary, the millionaire club-owner and ocean-racing yachtsman. They had flown to Antigua at de Savery's expense as guests of honour at the opening party he threw at his new St James's Club to which he invited an appreciable number of the world's wealthiest people. The Kents stayed for several days at the club – the sister of the elegant premises of the same name that de Savery had opened in London some years before.

The Kents' appearance there was regarded as a dubious commercial venture and did little to improve relations between Princess Michael and the royal family. And, as we have seen, it spawned a rumour that de Savary had given them a piece of land in Antigua in return for their services.

The party over, on 27 January, Prince and Princess Michael flew to Dallas where Prince Michael had business engagements for one of the four London companies that he represents.

They moved themselves into the Mansion on Turtle Creek, and early in the week Ward Hunt appeared. He came by appointment, driving a shooting-brake, and he was taking Princess Michael to a local horse event while Prince Michael carried on with his business.

Actually, the royal couple had hired a chauffeur for the entire trip. He said afterwards that Ward Hunt seemed keen on doing him out of a job, making frequent offers to drive the Princess around town. But Prince Michael insisted on independence, and retained the driver's services to take his wife shopping and the Prince to both his meeting and the local squash club.

The chauffeur also took them sightseeing to the chic Petroleum Club in the city, and the new multi-million-dollar Crescent Center that was being built by Ward Hunt's richer relatives. Courtesy of Ward Hunt, they paid a visit to a ranch owned by his cousin, Nelson Bunker Hunt, and they watched a rodeo in Fort Worth.

Fortuitously for the Princess, though, the Prince was due to have more business meetings, and a long way away. In New York. He had to be on the East Coast on Thursday, 31 January, and he decided to fly on the Wednesday evening as the weather forecast promised a huge snowstorm. He was concerned that he would be unable to land in New York. The original intention had been that his wife would leave with him. She had a better idea. She wanted to stay in Dallas. She told the Prince she would remain for one more night and then fly on to California in the morning.

The chauffeur arrived at the Mansion on Turtle Creek on 31 January at 6.30 in the morning. His instructions were to drive the Princess to the airport. She did not appear, and the plane went without her. It was just before noon when she swept into the lobby and said in her imperious way: 'Take me to the Terrace.'

Having had all that time to kill, he had noticed that the same instructions were also written in the hotel register against her name.

The Princess had the hotel porters place all her luggage in the limousine, and then she was driven to the Terrace, the luxury apartment-block in the leafy residential part of Dallas where only the very rich – and Ward Hunt – dwell. Afterwards the driver recalled: 'All her luggage was taken out of the car and placed in the foyer of the apartment-block. The porter took care of it.'

She then turned to her driver and said grandly: 'Your services are no longer required. You may dismiss.'

He dismissed. And, had she been less arrogant, perhaps he would have been less talkative when a *News of the World* reporter turned up barely six months later in his life.

The Princess made another private trip to America at the beginning of 1985. She went at the end of March or early in April. But she vanished into thin air once she arrived.

In May, when she went to California, she was more conspicuous. All of 1230 miles from Dallas, she and Ward Hunt spent several days alone. They were together 140 miles from Los Angeles at the 165-acre Hillview Farm, a ranch in the Californian hills, near to Santa Ynez and close to President Reagan's summer holiday home.

The two-bedroom, open-plan ranch-house belonged to one of Princess Michael's closest confidantes – Princess Esra Jah. Princess Esra is the daughter of the last Sultan of Turkey and she married the multi-millionaire Nizam of Hyderabad in 1960. He left her, first to run a sheep and cattle range in Western Australia, and eventually for a thirty-one-year-old Australian girl by whom he has a son. He divorced forty-five-year-old Esra in 1980 and, like Ward Hunt, he found it very expensive. The Princess prefers to live in her £250,000 house in Kensington, and she rarely visits the Californian ranch. It is in the care of a Mexican, Chico Francisco, and his Texan wife, Olga. They have a home in the grounds.

Chico had been convinced that the mystery pair who came to stay – they never introduced themselves – were newlyweds. The tall blonde woman he described sounded exactly like Princess Michael, and the photograph he was shown of Ward Hunt he identified immediately. 'I was never told their names,' he said, 'only that they were very close friends of Princess Esra and would be staying for a while.' He had the impression that the woman had been ill and needed to rest. 'I thought they were married. They looked close and happy together,' he said.

The couple's stay was spent mainly lazing on the wooden verandah of the house with iced drinks at their side. Occasionally they strolled arm in arm around the estate, enjoying the magnificent views, or they drove through the miles of empty countryside in a hired Ford station wagon.

Their evenings were spent alone in the house.

'One night they brought in a woman especially to cook for them,' Chico said. 'They had no visitors. They were alone except for our three horses and dogs.'

It was undoubtedly while they were enjoying this romantic interlude that they planned their next meeting. The Princess surely realized that her credibility must be

wearing thin after all the American trips she had made
since January. Even a husband as doting and indulgent
as Prince Michael would begin to ask questions. She was
brilliant at fobbing off his questions, but there was a
limit. . . .

Perhaps it was then that she and Hunt made the plan
to meet in London in June. Or maybe she believed that
somehow she would find an excuse to return to America
as quickly as possible so they could be together again. For
one thing is sure: she was in love with Hunt, and she was
laying her head on the block for him. Her problem was
that she was unable to accept the enormity of what she
was doing. Believing that she could get away with anything, she did not appreciate how dangerous a game she
was playing.

Whether Hunt's fateful trip to London was her suggestion, or whether he thought of it himself, is not known –
but the outcome was to be disaster for them both. Almost
as if to flaunt her affair, the Princess sent her husband off
alone to three ceremonial occasions the week before Hunt
arrived. She even declined an invitation from the Queen
to lunch at Windsor Castle during Ascot week. Some say
that no such invitation was sent; but it is unthinkable that
the Queen, who puts good manners before everything,
would have considered inviting Prince Michael without
inviting his wife. In the event, Prince Michael went alone
to the Queen's luncheon-party.

Princess Michael and Hunt spent four idyllic days together – two of them in a flat no more than a mile or two
from her Kensington Palace home, and the remainder in
the country. It was while they were in the country that
the Princess received a warning that her affair was no
longer a secret. The press had found out.

Though she did not know it, Princess Michael's world
had begun to collapse around her towards the end of
May, when the *News of the World* received information

that she was having an affair with an American. Rumours had been in the air for some time, but the identity of Princess Michael's 'friend' had not been established. Investigation now revealed the gentleman to be J. Ward Hunt. Further research filled in the Hunt family background, while the official programme for the American fund-raising tour on behalf of the English National Opera established a firm link between the guest of honour, Princess Michael, and fund-raiser and party host Ward Hunt of Dallas.

Then came a major development. It seemed that the Princess's attachment to Hunt had become so strong that she had asked him to come to Britain and spend a week with her in London. Those in royal circles who knew what was going on were appalled. They had indicated to the Princess that, if she must misbehave, she should do so a long way away. To bring the affair right on to her own doorstep was simply not on.

She had chosen to ignore the advice, and Hunt was due to arrive in London on Monday, 24 June. He had initially been booked into the Carlton Tower hotel, but that reservation had later been cancelled. He would now be staying in a private flat in Eaton Square owned by the brother of Princess Esra of Hyderabad. The couple would spend two days there before going to the country home of Rosie, Marchioness of Northampton in Moreton-in-the-Marsh for the remainder of the week.

Hunt left Dallas on an American Airlines flight on the afternoon of Sunday, 23 June, unaware that his progress was being closely followed all the way. Indeed, a reporter had not only succeeded in booking a ticket on the same flight, but had also managed to obtain the seat next to Hunt. However, despite attempts to engage him in conversation, Hunt said little and spent most of the flight asleep.

On arrival at Gatwick airport on the morning of 24

June, Hunt travelled by train to Victoria, where a taxi took him to Eaton Square. His arrival was observed by a *News of the World* reporter and photographer. Earlier, at 9.10, they had watched the arrival of a tall female wearing a beige calf-length trench-coat with the collar pulled up and headscarf drawn tightly round her face to obscure her features. She had arrived in a chauffeur-driven Mercedes with another woman, and carrying an overnight bag. The other woman left, but returned later with ten plastic carrier bags containing food and other provisions. The Princess and her friend had set up home in this most beautiful of London squares – no more than two miles or so from her own home and husband.

They stayed in the Eaton Square flat throughout Monday, 24 June; they were there that night; and they were there the following morning. Princess Michael, Ward Hunt and Princess Esra, who had returned to the flat, left shortly after midday on the Tuesday, 25 June. The Princess was wearing a curly red wig.

The *News of the World* reporters needed evidence to confirm that the woman in the red wig was indeed Princess Michael. Their photographs were not in themselves conclusive proof. Hoping that the chauffeur would be able to identify his passenger, they set about tracing the driver of the Mercedes. He turned out to be Donald Lightbody, who lived in north London. Mr Lightbody was discreet. He refused to discuss the matter, though he did eventually agree that the car in the photographs was his and that he had been the driver. However, his wife accidentally let slip that her husband's passenger had been a member of the royal family, with a strong hint that she was Princess Michael.

Edging closer to a positive identification of the woman at the flat, the Editor of the *News of the World* suggested they might be able to identify the overnight bag as belonging to the Princess. An exhaustive search of the picture files almost ended in defeat, until someone remembered a batch of very recent photographs which had not yet been added to the files. Among them was a picture of Princess Michael carrying the very distinctive bag that could be seen in the Eaton Square photographs.

That Tuesday, 25 June, had been an awkward day for the Princess, for she had two long-standing commitments – both with her husband. She was obliged to break away from her Texan friend.

The earlier of the two engagements was a Freemasons' reception for members and their wives in the crypt of the Guildhall. Prince Michael is an active Mason; he was the Master of the Grand Steward's Lodge for 1985. His elder brother, the Duke of Kent, is Grand Master – Britain's foremost Mason. The reception, held primarily for the ladies' benefit, started at six o'clock in the evening and went on until eight. The Prince and Princess stayed to the end. She was in sparkling form – as well she might be, exhilarated by the danger of the deception.

She was unable to escape immediately. From the reception the couple went on to a private party for twenty-four people which was being given for the American ambassador by Prince Rupert Lowenstein. It took place at the fashionable Mark's Club, where Prince Charles gave his pre-wedding party.

Suddenly the Princess said that she wanted to make a move before the other guests. She told her husband that she was leaving that night for the country house of her great friend Rosie, Marchioness of Northampton, and she had the excuse of the long drive to the Cotswolds. She was telling the truth. She *was* going to the Cotswolds – but she was not going alone.

While the Princess was otherwise engaged, Ward Hunt spent the evening dining at the Savoy Grill with a party of Americans. His host, the *News of the World* discovered later, was Ronald Driver, the chairman of

143

London United Investments. Hunt was delivered back to the Eaton Square flat at around 11.30 p.m. As we have seen, Prince Michael is a director of Ronald Driver's company.

While the Lowenstein party was still in full swing, Princess Michael left and returned to Kensington Palace to change from her beautiful dress into something less conspicuous. Then, driving herself in a small car and wearing her red wig and long coat, she went back to the Eaton Square flat. Later, she and her Texan friend left to drive to the home of Rosie, Marchioness of Northampton. And there they stayed for two days, without apparently leaving the house and grounds.

Events took an altogether dramatic turn on the Friday, 28 June. The Princess somehow received word that the press were on to her. How she found out is still a mystery, but the news caused her to panic. There were desperate conferences with Ward Hunt, and he was smartly sent packing.

Hunt returned to Dallas a bruised man. He had offered to marry his Princess, but she had refused him. He had conceived a plan. He wanted to take her back to Texas and make her his Queen. It would have been the ultimate achievement in Dallas, where status means everything. To bring a British princess back as his bride could have been the triumph of his life. But more than prestige was involved. He was very much in love. He was bewitched by the Princess, enchanted by her as she had enchanted many. Indeed, as she enchanted Prince Michael himself.

However, he was left alone to lick his wounds, while his Princess concentrated on saving her skin for the second time that year. Her first and only thought was to devise some plan to extricate herself from the dreadful situation in which she had landed herself.

She came up with the idea that she should appear to

have suffered a nervous breakdown (and at that moment she had every reason to have one!). She rang her doctor and said she wished to be admitted to a clinic at once.

'But there has to be something wrong with you,' her doctor said.

'I'm having a nervous breakdown,' she told him.

At the same time she had to ensure that Hunt left the country as quickly as possible. Faced with the final decision, with steely logic she had decided that a princess at Kensington Palace was better than a queen of a Dallas palace, regardless of the differences in the bank balances of the two men in her life. But, then, she had discovered as the weeks and months went by that Hunt was not in the same financial class as some of her other friends.

Princess Michael is close to many wealthy men. One is the Italian industrialist, Dr Marino Chiavelli, a staggeringly rich international entrepreneur who made his vast fortune by secretly procuring oil for South Africa in spite of international embargoes. He is said to have been very helpful to the Prince and Princess – particularly at the time when they were trying to raise money for Nether Lypiatt Manor, their home in the Cotswolds. The doctor – who has convictions in his native Italy for passing worthless cheques and fraudulently calling himself 'doctor' – is the kind of contact that sends shudders down the royal family's collective spine. He is not a pretty man, but he is very rich, and rumour has it that he did once buy the Princess a Rolls-Royce. It was not the grandest model, so word is that she sold it.

One of her other rich friends is more socially acceptable – the American banker, oilman and horse-breeder, eighty-seven-year-old John Galbreath. After a visit to his Columbus, Ohio, headquarters in the summer of 1984, Galbreath, an enormously wealthy man, presented the Princess with a two-year-old filly named Spirit of the Wind. Worth $150,000, it was a staggeringly generous gift. Clearly the Princess made a great hit with Galbreath.

Hunt could not compete financially with these friends. It was unfortunate for both of them, but she had had to accept that Hunt was not the catch of the century. At this moment of truth, she turned down his proposal of marriage and told him it was time to call it a day. She also told him to get out of England as fast as he could. Not surprisingly, Hunt was shattered.

She now had to sell her nervous breakdown idea to Buckingham Palace. At ten o'clock that morning she told her unofficial lady-in-waiting that she wanted a statement on those lines issued to the press. Anne Frost baulked at the suggestion and there was a great deal of telephoning from Moreton to Kensington Palace between her and the unfortunate Colonel Farmer, who was going to have to sort it all out. She was determined to say that she was suffering from nervous exhaustion, caused by the revelations of two months before that her father had a Nazi background. She intended immediately to cancel all further engagements. She felt that this was a good pre-emptive, sympathy-gaining move. If any newspaper were to publish a report about her friendship with Hunt, the public would once again rally to her side as they had rallied over the Nazi story.

Colonel Farmer referred to the Palace for advice.

Later that morning, the Princess set out for London. She was unsure of her own plans, fearing that her marriage might be at crisis-point, nervous about whether she should drive directly to the home of her good friend Anne Frost, also known as 'Jumbo', who by chance lived next door to Nigel Dempster, Britain's most celebrated gossip columnist.

She was due back at Kensington Palace for a long-standing engagement at 2.30 that afternoon. She was meant to leave at that time with Prince Michael for a function that evening, the Soldiers', Sailors' and Airmen's Families Association tattoo which was taking place in the grounds of Blenheim Palace, Oxfordshire – just a few miles from where she had been staying.

The suggestion given to her by royal advisers was to do nothing other than carry on normally. Princess Michael was not in the business of taking advice. She was convinced that for her she knew what was best. Knowing what was best had, after all, brought her from a working girl's life in Sydney to Kensington Palace. By 2.30 that afternoon she was installed in the Sister Agnes Clinic at the King Edward VII Hospital for Officers in Marylebone, the small and extremely exclusive private hospital used by the royal family, usually for minor surgical operations.

Events here become a little fudged. One school of thought says that Prince Michael went with her to the hospital. Another says he did nothing of the kind but went off to do his duty for the SSAFA and that her 'lady-in-waiting' accompanied her. He most certainly was at Blenheim Palace that night, but as for whether he dropped his wife into hospital nobody but the participants seems to know.

With the *fait accompli* of the Princess being safely tucked up in bed, the debate between royal private secretaries and press secretaries was reduced to deciding what kind of public statement to make. And it continued for some hours. There was considerable discussion as to the exact wording that should be used to describe something that most certainly wasn't a classic nervous breakdown. The royal advisers, always preferring to skate around a situation rather than be caught telling big black lies, had a problem. And, as the argument went on, the only person who was not consulted was Prince Michael.

Prince Michael, as husbands usually are, was the last to know.

That night the Princess ended the debate herself by demanding that Colonel Farmer issue a statement. It was late because, while Princess Michael was popping herself into hospital, he was stuck in a traffic jam on the way to visit an ancient uncle in Oxfordshire. Much against his better judgement he did what she wished. It was very simple, merely saying that she was going into the hospital for a period of rest and had cancelled her immediate engagements. 'Ever since then people have been asking me what I meant by "immediate",' says Michael Farmer. 'It was a difficult one....'

Later another statement was made by Buckingham Palace. Because it was issued over a weekend, there is no record on paper, no date, no time, but the Palace recall that the statement went something like: 'We confirm that the Princess has had to go into hospital for a period of rest.'

While all this was happening, Hunt was scurrying from England. A private helicopter hired from Dollar Helicopters of Coventry took him from Moreton-in-the-Marsh to Manchester Ringway airport to catch the 2 p.m. British Airways flight to New York, with a linking flight to Dallas that same night. On the last leg of his journey the luckless Hunt again had a reporter for company. On this occasion he was more talkative. He admitted that he had been friendly with the Prince and Princess since first meeting them in Dallas two years earlier. When told that the Princess had been admitted to hospital suffering from nervous exhaustion, Hunt appeared concerned and said that he knew – friends had told him – that the Princess had been feeling the strain of the press revelations about her father's Nazi past. When asked directly whether he had seen the Princess while in Britain he replied: 'No, it was a business trip.' The reporter then told him of the *News of the World*'s investigation and of the evidence of his liaison with Princess Michael. Hunt refused to say more, though he seemed surprised at the trouble the newspaper had taken with the story and remarked: 'This is the closest thing to James Bond I've ever met.'

On the following Monday, Hunt issued a brief statement through his secretary:

> Princess Michael is a friend of the Hunt family. As far as these rumours are concerned, they are totally unfounded. That is all I have to say.

There he was back at home, and there was she in hospital, enjoying a whole new wave of public sympathy.

With banks of cameras stationed outside the hospital, the press was very much in evidence when the Princess's children came to visit her on Saturday. It was a scene heavy with emotion. Four-year-old Lady Gabriella was carrying Mummy's favourite pink teddy bear, and also a posy of pink and white roses. Her six-year-old brother, Lord Frederick, had a small bouquet of yellow roses. Their father was not with them. They arrived in a car driven by their nanny.

'Mummy's all right,' said the little Lord poignantly as he and his sister left after a forty-minute visit. The cameramen and reporters, who had been stationed outside the hospital for hours, were having a bit of a problem with nervous exhaustion themselves.

The next day, Sunday, was the Princess's seventh wedding anniversary. Her husband came to see her in the evening, having spent most of the day at Blenheim Palace with the Marlboroughs. The press seemed to miss his arrival, but a rather tetchy Colonel Farmer assured the world the following morning that 'The Prince did go to the hospital'.

No other member of the royal family went near her.

The *News of the World* had still not published a word. The Princess's heart must have lifted when she read the issue of the newspaper for that Sunday, 30 June. It occu-

149

pied itself with Prince Charles's tumble from a polo pony, and she would have congratulated herself that perhaps her sympathy ploy had worked. Perhaps she was in the clear. She deserved a little luck.

Alternatively, she may have learned from the Palace of a communication they had received the previous day, 29 June. Still too cautious to publish the story until he was completely sure, the editor of the *News of the World* decided to address some direct questions to the Princess through John Haslam, a Buckingham Palace Press Secretary. The eight questions related to her relationship with Ward Hunt, and specifically to their meeting in Britain the previous week, and cited names, places, dates and times, and ended by asking for a statement 'as to the present state of the marriage of Their Royal Highnesses Prince and Princess Michael'.

It was a splendid piece of barefaced cheek, and the *News of the World* knew perfectly well that they would not receive the answers they required, but their cards were now on the table.

The Palace reply was brief – and by telephone. John Haslam merely said:

> Prince and Princess Michael had met Mr Hunt on a handful of occasions. Mr Hunt was not a fellow-guest when the Princess stayed in Oxfordshire during the week. Any suggestion other than that they are acquaintances is unfounded.

On 3 July, with its tongue firmly in its cheek, the *Sun* reported that 'Brave Prince Michael of Kent last night put aside his worries over his wife's health to go to his 43rd birthday party'. It was a party thrown for him by Lady Annabel Goldsmith at her home at Ham Common. Apart from refusing to answer questions about his wife's health, the Prince appeared to be in reasonably good form – all things considered.

On 5 July the Princess left hospital, without make-up, hair pulled severely straight back from her face, and wearing a dress with an innocent white Puritan collar. Her husband was waiting for her and, as the *Daily Star* put it, 'she went straight into his arms'. And once inside the black Daimler, while the cameras were still whirring, she leaned across to kiss him, before going home to an 'emotional reunion' with her children.

Having spent a week consolidating their information, on Sunday, 7 July, the *News of the World* published the story. 'ROYAL LOVE SENSATION (EXCLUSIVE OF THE YEAR),' said the front-page headline. 'PRINCESS MICHAEL TORN BETWEEN PRINCE AND HER DALLAS MILLIONAIRE.' Inside, across a double-page spread, it read: 'Wearing a wig, she keeps a late-night rendezvous at a friend's flat in Belgravia.' Below: 'World Exclusive! ROYAL LOVE AGONY. SECRET MEETING PLACES FOR MICHAEL AND HER DALLAS TYCOON.' Chapter and verse for all the garnered material was there.

But the newspaper still had words of comfort for the Princess:

> While the curiosity of the public can be irritating to bear, the love of the public can be moving to behold.
> For the Princess there is a strong arm of affection on which she can lean.

Perhaps she did not need too much comfort. David Montgomery, the editor of the *News of the World*, was astonished to receive a letter on Kensington Palace headed paper. Dated 24 July 1985, it read:

> Dear Sir,
> Princess Michael of Kent has asked me to write to you to enquire whether the original Zoke cartoon on page 8 of the issue of the *News of the World* on 14th July, 1985 is still available.

151

If this is the case, I should be most grateful if you would kindly let me know the cost involved.

Thanking you in advance for your help in this matter.

Yours faithfully,
VERLA FREEMAN
Secretary

The cartoon in question pictured Prince and Princess Michael lounging on the deck of the yacht *Jessica* surrounded by newspapers headlined 'Princess and Dallas Tycoon', 'Princess and Nazi Father'. The caption had Prince Michael saying to the Princess: 'Now, are you sure you've nothing else to tell me, darling?' The Princess had been drawn with a mermaid's tail.

David Montgomery replied: 'I am delighted that Princess Michael of Kent liked the "Zoke" cartoon in the *News of the World* on July 14th, and I am pleased to enclose the original at no charge.' Cheekily, he added: 'I wrote to Colonel Farmer some time ago requesting an interview with Princess Michael. Perhaps the Princess would now be interested in doing this with us, and I would be happy if you contacted me personally to make the arrangements.'

A good try – but it didn't work. Her Royal Highness was delighted to receive the cartoon. With regard to the request for an interview she was still unwilling.

The request was a bizarre ending to an equally bizarre story.

Chapter 7

Princess Michael and the Dudleys

THE SUNDAY NEWSPAPERS were full of Princess Michael stories on the morning of 7 July 1985. The *News of the World* had gone to town with five full pages about the Princess's friendship with Ward Hunt. The *Mail on Sunday* had another and different aspect to 'the secret anguish of Princess Michael'. No, it was nothing to do with her problems with the Texan millionaire. This was a document which, said the *Mail*, revealed an amazing vendetta. The story read:

> An extraordinary document which friends of Princess Michael of Kent believe is the key to a campaign of hostility against her has come into the possession of the *Mail on Sunday*.
>
> It is an apology, written in the most grovelling

terms to her by a leading member of the aristocracy.

It comes from the Earl of Dudley and was written just before Christmas 1983.

The apology states – 'I write on behalf of my wife and myself to place on record the most sincere regret for the grave distress and embarrassment which we have caused you, Princess Michael, and your family and we unreservedly express our deep apologies. We acknowledge the statements were untruthful and never should have been made.

I also undertake that there will be delivery to Sir Max Williams of all copies of the poems which are within my possession or power and in addition where possible from those to whom we have supplied copies.'

The letter was signed 'Dudley', and dated 17 December 1983.

Sir Max Williams was Princess Michael's solicitor, and the *Mail* said that 'the apology was forced out of the Earl of Dudley after he had circulated a scurrilous poem about Princess Michael' – a poem that apparently Princess Michael believed was the start of all her troubles. This piece of literature, it seemed, was responsible for the allegations that her marriage was threatened. And, *ipso facto*, why she had become involved with another man in the first place.

This was the latest episode in the long-running saga of the Earl, his Countess, the Princess and the naughty poem; a saga that had crept into the press only in dribs and drabs, but one that had kept all of high society riveted for many a long month.

The Earl of Dudley was extremely angry that the letter had been 'leaked'. The apology had only been written to satisfy the Princess's honour, and strictly on the promise that it was never made public. Now, on the very day that Princess Michael was in really deep trouble, there was the Earl's abject apology printed in black and white. Would it encourage yet a little more public sympathy for the poor, hard-done-by Princess? Someone obviously thought so. A someone who had time to think long and hard about how to deflect the revelations that the *News of the World* were about to spring on the public. Princess Michael, of course, had been languishing in her hospital bed until two days before. But someone had handed a copy of the private apology to the *Mail on Sunday*, probably on the Friday or Saturday.

The poem had been written as the result of a sharp clash between Princess Michael and the Countess of Dudley. The Earl has published poetry about flowers and nature, but this poem was different. It was witty, decidedly barbed, and perceptive. And it was no wonder that Princess Michael was distraught when she eventually read the poem herself. It went into detail about her father's wartime past. It would have mentioned that the Baron von Reibnitz had been in the SS if Lord Dudley could have found a rhyme for SS. It told what the Princess got up to in the cinema with Elizabeth Taylor's ex-husband, Senator John Warner, and it had a lot of pertinent things to say about her extravagant character, her personality and her ambitions.

It was, of course, scurrilous. Unfortunately for the Princess, it was also very funny, so funny that Princess Margaret is said to have fallen off her chair laughing when she heard it.

The poem was such a howling success that copies began to be circulated, not only in Britain but on the Continent as well. This was a development Lord Dudley says was never intended.

> I wrote the poem to cheer up my wife who was very upset by what had happened with Princess Michael. It was not meant for general circulation and was just shown to a few close friends. Unfortunately

somebody thought it was so good that they distributed it to a wider readership.

The Earl was furious not only that the apology for the poem had been leaked but also by the *Mail on Sunday*'s inference that he was orchestrating a vendetta against the Princess. It seemed as if he were being made a scapegoat for the whole range of Princess Michael's indiscretions.

> There is no vendetta against the Prince and Princess. In fact, they would be the first to acknowledge the fact. It appears that the document containing my apology was released by the Princess – or someone close to her – for three reasons.
>
> It created a smokescreen to explain her hospitalization, to gain sympathy for the Princess and to find a scapegoat.

He insisted to reporter Andrew Morton that the apology was only sent in the truly grovelling form that it was as a face-saver for the Princess.

> The letter was sent just before Christmas when the Michaels (sic) were due to spend the holiday with the Queen at Windsor. The poem has been seen by members of the Royal family and the Princess wanted a face-saver to show them.
>
> On that basis it was sent. It was meant to be private and would never have been written in this way if it were to appear in the Press.
>
> It should have been kept under lock and key at Kensington Palace.

The Earl has a letter from Sir Max Williams to his own solicitor, Lord Goodman. The letter, dated 20 December, gave assurances that Princess Michael and her husband would disclose the letter only to those who read the poem or were acquainted with its material contents.

Lord Dudley says that, knowing the Princess's track record, he had reservations about writing the apology at all.

He said: 'At the same time I wrote the apology, I also wrote a personal letter to the Princess explaining the surroundings and the circumstances and the strong emotions I felt at the time which had led me to write the poem.'

But what could have caused all this fluttering in the social dovecotes? Why was the sixty-five-year-old Earl so angry with Princess Michael? What had she done to his wife to make her so upset that she was, says the Earl, in tears?

The full story will probably never be known as the protagonists and those closest to them are naturally unwilling or reluctant to discuss the affair in detail and what has emerged would never have been investigated or unearthed but for the interest aroused by the belated and unexpected publication of the Earl's apology. Some account of the events can, however, be pieced together from press accounts, from friends of those involved or from references to the public appearances of the Princess and the Countess during the United States trip and afterwards.

The story began in October 1982 when the Princess and the Countess met through mutual friends, including the society hostess, Fleur Cowles.

Lady Dudley and the Princess became very good friends. They had a lot in common; both were interested in the arts, in ballet, in decoration. Both were very knowledgeable about these subjects. At the same time the Princess's friendship with Fleur Cowles also blossomed.

Then, it seemed, Fleur Cowles had a brainwave. She remembered a conversation with two American designer friends, Jerry Silverman and Sherren Rodgers. They had a dream about opening a fashion school at Kent State University in Ohio. Fleur hit upon the idea of organizing a visit to the University by Prince and Princess Michael. An appearance by the royal Kents to the identically named University had a touch of style. It would not be a problem to arrange as Prince and Princess Michael were already paying a visit to the Gateway to Britain exhibition in Columbus, Ohio, and both events were being organized by Fleur Cowles.

It was she who was making all the arrangements. But the trip seems to have been doomed from the start. Princess Grace died in Monaco, and Fleur Cowles went to the funeral. While in Monaco, Miss Cowles, who is far from being a young woman, broke her leg. Princess Michael asked her friend, the Countess of Dudley, if she would take Fleur Cowles' place and act as a sort of unofficial lady-in-waiting. Princess Michael is not important enough in the royal pecking order to be entitled to a lady-in-waiting, but she likes to have someone in attendance. Her friends do often indulge her in this little bit of vanity.

As it happened, Maureen Dudley was planning a trip to America to see one of her five daughters, Lady Susanna Ward, who was studying at Columbia University in New York. But the nature of the trip began to change.

Princess Michael telephoned Maureen at the Dudleys' country home in Devon and invited the Countess to join her on a trip, starting with a flight on Concorde to New York, moving to Ohio by small private plane and then back to Washington. It began to sound like a lot of fun. The Countess thought that travelling in America with her good friend the Princess was a bonus on top of the proposed visit to Lady Susanna.

Yet before they even set off there was another problem looming. The Kents' secretary, John Barratt, was beginning to crack up under the strain of the job, and with Fleur Cowles out of action he was left to make all the arrangements for the trip. In the normal way, Barratt, a quiet man of considerable charm, is highly efficient. But he was not used to the mercurial temperament of Princess Michael. Lord Mountbatten had been demanding, but when arrangements were made they stayed made, and if Lord Mountbatten had an engagement he kept it.

He had agreed that Princess Michael with Lady Dudley would go to a fund-raising dinner given by an enormously wealthy American. They were also engaged for a reception at the Brazilian embassy in Washington.

To add to Barratt's problems, while arrangements were still being slotted together the Princess suddenly announced she wanted to go to the New York opening of *Cats* and also demanded that arrangements be made for her to be received in Washington – she wanted a miniature royal tour – and in the middle of all the preparations she suddenly disappeared to Austria for a few days.

When she returned, just hours before the trip was to begin, she had changed her mind, and instructed John Barratt to 'get her out' of the Brazilian embassy dinner.

Everyone tried to talk her out of 'chucking' the Brazilian embassy, but she had a great excuse. She said: 'It's because of the Falklands. You know, Brazil, South America. I can't go to the Brazilian embassy. They are on the other side.'

At the end of the day, though, reason prevailed. She agreed to go. No one has ever worked out the reason for her reluctance. It was, after all, just another hot dinner for the Princess.

Maureen Dudley set off first for America. She spent a weekend in New York with her daughter and then the Sunday Concorde from London brought the Princess, Prince Michael and their secretary, John Barratt, into Kennedy Airport. The two women greeted each other affectionately, the Princess towering over the petite, dark-haired Countess, who, in her youth, as Maureen Swanson had been a successful ballet dancer and actress.

Their first event was Mary Lee Fairbanks's charity first night of Andrew Lloyd Webber's show, *Cats*. Mary Lee Fairbanks is a famous hostess, wife of Sir Douglas Fairbanks, and a friend of the Queen. The Princess was outraged when she found that Mary Lee had seated her and

Maureen Dudley next to two American men in the theatre. 'I am not going to sit next to Americans,' she informed her startled (American) hostess. 'I have only come here to support British charities. Have the seating arrangements changed.' Two substitute Englishmen were hastily found.

She never did go to the Brazilian embassy dinner. Her party arrived late, and as they came into the reception room *folie de grandeur* struck again. Friends say she was heard to shout angrily at Maureen Dudley: 'You have allowed guests to leave before me.'

Not too delighted herself with this display, Maureen Dudley said through clenched teeth: 'What did you want me to do? Hold them down?'

The Princess did not reply. She just swept out of the Brazilian embassy and got into her car and drove off.

Maureen Dudley was experiencing what the hired help normally had to deal with. There was no hired help to take the brunt. Not too surprisingly, John Barratt was not with them. He had collapsed almost as soon as they had arrived and was in hospital in New York. He was found slumped half out of his bed in the elegant Carlyle Hotel where the group were staying and taken to a New York hospital.

The Princess's temper continued uncertain throughout the trip. Next stop was Cleveland, Ohio, where it was decided at Prince Michael's suggestion that some apologies were in order. The Princess sulkily agreed when she learned that Mary Lee Fairbanks was a friend of the Queen. It was in Ohio that the Princess met John Galbreath, the tycoon and horsebreeder. She heard that Galbreath did not live too far away, and she buttonholed the British consul-general at a reception and asked if he could fix up a meeting. She spent the afternoon with this elderly gentleman before going on to an event in the evening at six o'clock. Rumour is that she flirted outrageously, and fact is that he gave her a racehorse.

Princess Michael riding side-saddle on her horse, State Occasion.
Nether Lypiatt Manor is in the background

Top: the family with their pet goats, Donna and Lucy, named after the characters in *Dallas*, a favourite television show

Above: ready for a fancy dress ball

Right: Lord and Lady of the Manor

Top left: relaxing in Barbados, following the trip to Antigua to open Peter de Savary's club

Top right: with Michael Harfield, one-time priest and Marie-Christine's confessor, now turned Sydney PR man

Above: one of Princess Michael's less glamorous engagements – opening a Happy Eater restaurant on the A3 in Surrey

Above: a hat to suit every mood
Right: the stunning but controversial fortieth birthday portrait

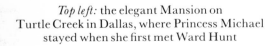

Top left: the elegant Mansion on
Turtle Creek in Dallas, where Princess Michael
stayed when she first met Ward Hunt

Top right: Princess Michael with Ward Hunt

Above: Hillview Farm, the hideaway
Princess Michael and Ward Hunt used in California

Right: Princess Michael returning from
California carrying her overnight bag

Top left: 75 Eaton Square

Top right: Princess Michael arrives at
Eaton Square with the fateful bag

Above: Ward Hunt joins the Princess
at the Eaton Square flat

bove right: the Princess looking very drawn
as she leaves her hospital sanctuary
to be collected by Prince Michael

Right: reunited with her husband

Top: at Wimbledon, two days after leaving hos

Left: steering in calmer waters, aboard
the *Jessica* in the Mediterranean

Above: with Jerry Hall and Marie Helvin
at a fashion gala

The Princess got her trip to Washington, but Prince Michael had to return to London for business reasons. The Earl of Dudley agreed to join the two women, and he flew from London at his own expense, stopping off in New York to visit John Barratt in hospital. As usual the publicity machine to ensure that the Princess was received in the style to which she had become accustomed had gone into action. Arianna Stassinopoulos the writer, television personality and former lady-friend of Bernard Levin, had been given the job of making the arrangements. Hers fared no better than John Barratt's. The first night there was to be a big dinner-party to welcome the Princess, then she was to attend the ballet at the Kennedy Centre, and Maureen Dudley herself fixed hostess parties at the homes of her friends. There was no shortage of wealthy American women who would lay on tea-parties, cocktail-parties, dinner-parties for the privilege of saying that they had entertained a member of the British royal family in their own homes.

Most of the arrangements that Arianna had made were dumped. Princess Michael thought there was more fun to be had elsewhere. She was prepared to go to the ballet, accompanied by the British ambassador, Sir Oliver Wright, but Sir Oliver asked Lady Dudley if he could have the night off. He would greatly appreciate it, he said, as his grandchildren were visiting and he so rarely saw them. Lady Dudley agreed. At which point the relieved ambassador took himself off, after assuring the Dudleys that supper would be laid on for their party at the embassy for ten o'clock.

Here was the root of the tension between the two women. When Maureen Dudley said she had given the ambassador the night off, Princess Michael, enraged that anyone else should give what she thought of as orders, exploded, demanding to know what right Lady Dudley had to interfere with the plans.

The ambassador, she insisted, was there to serve her.

She stormed off to phone the ambassador, but returned later, all smiles. She had found herself another escort. John Warner, Elizabeth Taylor's husband, who was just one month from divorce from the flamboyant actress.

'Guess who I've got coming to the ballet,' she said smugly. 'Senator John Warner. He's very famous.'

It seemed that Princess Michael was delighted by the Elizabeth Taylor connection. She liked the idea of being escorted by the man who had married one of the most fascinating women in the world.

They were to meet at a reception given by a Washington socialite. It seemed that the Princess was too excited by the thought of her date that night to eat. She looked at the magnificent table laden with smoked salmon and champagne and said: 'I had smoked salmon for lunch. I couldn't eat any more.'

There was a discussion going on among the group about a French film that was showing at a suburban cinema in Washington. The Princess became fixed on the idea that she would rather see that than go to the ballet. John Warner had arrived, and after some discussion it was agreed that they must go to the ballet. They pointed out that everyone was expecting to see the Princess there.

She had cheered up a good deal when the Senator arrived. Her famous smile was back once she saw her date for the evening, and his eyes lit up at the sight of her. Warner is a good-looking man with presence, and she did not seem to have any objections to being on his arm for the evening. Even if he was American.

The auditorium was brilliantly lit at the theatre, and every eye in the house was on the Princess and her escort. Within a few minutes, the couple were sitting closer than convention allowed and when the curtain came down after the first act the Princess stood up and announced: 'We're leaving.'

The Dudleys could not believe their ears.

'But you can't,' Maureen Dudley protested. 'It's insulting to the embassy and the ballet.'

Princess Michael did not appear to be interested in the Embassy. She announced, 'I am going.'

The embarrassed Dudleys had little choice other than to leave, too.

The Princess was determined to go to the cinema to see the French film, and John Warner had some idea where it was. They made their way there in the embassy car, all in full dress, diamonds and taffeta sweeping skirts, the men in dinner-jackets. There was an hour and a half before the film was due to start, and for a while they just drove round and round. Washington is not a night-time city. It dies at eight o'clock. Then John Warner said he had thought of somewhere they could get a drink. He knew the owner of one of Washington's less salubrious hamburger joints and he persuaded the man to open up for the four of them. The Princess, the Countess, the Earl and the Senator, who also happened still to be Elizabeth Taylor's husband, all piled in, leaving the embassy car and the chauffeur outside. It was an undignified and embarrassing situation, and the Dudleys were wishing themselves a million miles away.

Nothing improved in the cinema. Maureen Dudley had said it would be a good idea to have a pact and leave after an hour if the film was boring. It was agreed. But, once in the darkness, John Warner was not paying too much attention to the screen. He and the Princess were re-experiencing their lost youth in the back row.

The Dudleys stood it for half an hour, and then Lady Dudley said she had a headache and thought they should go.

John Warner agreed. Princess Michael imperiously told him to stay.

Warner stayed.

The Dudleys went back to the embassy, ate the lobster

supper that had been left for them and went to bed as quickly as possible.

Came the morning, Princess Michael was in a rage.

'I did not give Billy permission to leave,' she hissed at Maureen Dudley, who later said to friends that she could not believe her ears. Her husband had come to Washington at his own expense, he was most certainly not on the Princess's staff – she wasn't even entitled to a lady-in-waiting – and she was saying she hadn't given the Earl of Dudley permission to leave. Making matters worse, she went on: 'I sent the butler up to get Billy to come down and sit with us. But he didn't come. I had to keep the butler up all night to chaperon us in the drawing-room.'

There were a lot of things that Lady Dudley might have said had she not been speechless. Like why did they sit up all night? Why didn't Warner go home and let the Princess go to bed?

A much-recovered John Barratt rejoined them in Washington just as the trip was about to end, and wanted to know how the visit had gone. He was still confused. His first instructions on arriving had been to change Princess Michael's flights. She was going to spend an extra weekend in the United States.

Barratt asked Lady Dudley if everything had gone well in Washington. She told him the full story, feeling that, if there were repercussions, forewarned was forearmed. It was a mistake. Out of some sense of loyalty, Barratt promptly repeated what had been said back to his employer. Her mood with Lady Dudley was instantly cooler.

The next on the list to feel her wrath was a local hair-dresser. He was thrilled to bits at the thought of working on a princess's hair. Unfortunately, he was a couple of minutes late.

'You are late for me,' roared the angry Princess. 'Too late. No one ever keeps me waiting.'

He left almost in tears.

At a store that night where British goods were on display, something had gone wrong with the arrangements. There was no champagne. The Princess's displeasure showed, and eventually Lady Dudley asked a rather nervous store director if they could have something to drink. He sent out for some white wine. It was warm. The Princess was angry.

'I am not going to drink warm white wine,' she declared.

She crushed the store director in the presence of the British consul-general. The press had started to ask questions as she left. The director was unwise enough to try to answer one of them. She turned on him. 'Are you giving this interview or am I?' she asked.

That night she received a phone call from a Mr Warren. She was booked, and left, on the 7.45 a.m. flight to New York. At 8.30 the hotel switchboard put through a call to Lady Dudley's room. It was a man, asking if Princess Michael had left. Maureen Dudley asked who was calling and was told: 'A friend.'

'Then, I'm sorry but I can't tell you,' she said.

There was a thoughtful pause and then the caller said: 'Mr Warren.'

Maureen Dudley said she did not know a Mr Warren. She did say later that the caller sounded exactly like John Warner, and that it wasn't a very difficult anagram to solve.

Certainly Princess Michael spent that weekend in New York, and certainly John Warner was in town, too. And there was, at the end of the day, some dispute about the bill at the Carlyle Hotel. The trip had had disastrous moments from start to finish.

But the repercussions were to go on. A few weeks later Nigel Dempster printed an item about how tongues were wagging in Washington about how well the Princess and

John Warner had got on. The Princess, still not accepting that indiscreet behaviour is always highly noted and by many, accused Maureen Dudley of planting the item. She also told a close friend that Lady Dudley had had far too much to drink and had behaved atrociously. And she said very much the same thing to the Earl.

'But, Ma'am, Maureen hardly drinks at all,' the Earl protested and changed the subject.

If there was any orchestrated vendetta at this stage of the drama, it was all directed against the Countess of Dudley. She was accused of upsetting a girl employee at the British embassy over a tip, of having been tipsy, told she would never be welcome at the British embassy again and that she had not appreciated the consul-general's efforts to help when the party was in Ohio. Indeed, she had been rude to the British consul. It is possible that she may not have been her usual amusing self. She must have become more and more edgy as the trip progressed. The whole affair has the fraught feeling of walking a tightrope with a bed of eggs underneath.

And it was at this point, when society was buzzing with the tale of the disagreement between the Countess and the Princess, that the Earl wrote his poem.

And soon afterwards John Barratt sent a letter to Princess Michael. Why he did so is hard to understand. There was no need for him to become involved; he had been in hospital when the Washington affair had been going on. He had never seen Princess Michael with John Warner. But on 12 June he wrote to tell her of his surprise and distress on learning that she had been accused of inventing a story about Lady Dudley's behaviour at the British Embassy in Washington.

He went on to say that the facts were that the ambassador had been delighted to have the Princess at the embassy and hoped she would soon return. He then went on to confirm the current gossip about the incident involving

166

Lady Dudley and the embassy social secretary, plus the remarks of the British consul-general in Ohio.

Eventually, a copy of the letter found its way to Lord and Lady Dudley, and in a most curious manner. They happened to bump into the publisher Lord Weidenfeld at a party. He is a friend of Princess Michael's; he is also publishing her first book when it is eventually written.

Lord Weidenfeld said he had a letter that would put everything right between the Princess and the Countess. They could be friends again. Surely, he could not have read it, for when it turned up from the Weidenfeld offices about a week later, postmarked 23 June 1983, it was the letter that John Barratt had written, assuring the Princess that she had behaved in an exemplary manner and that the mote was in the eye of Lady Dudley.

The Dudleys, noted their friends, were enraged, as much by the means by which they had received the letter as by the wording itself. They immediately took advice from their solicitor, Lord Goodman. The distinguished lawyer recommended that it was a situation where no action was the best action.

Lord Dudley, determined to end the situation once and for all, took himself off to confront John Barratt at his home in Surrey. Barratt was in the garden, and not a little surprised to see the broad frame of the Earl bearing down on him.

'Hello, Billy, what on earth are you doing here?' he said when Lord Dudley appeared over the garden fence.

Dudley said he had come for a serious talk, and Barratt said he had better come into the house.

Indoors, they discussed the letter, and Lord Dudley has since told friends that John Barratt admitted to him that it had been written as the result of a telephone call from Princess Michael. Eventually, Barratt was supposed to have agreed to retract the letter. It never happened.

As he was leaving, Lord Dudley asked why the letter had ever been written. John Barratt replied by saying that he had worked for many years with Lord Mountbatten, and Dickie had taught him one thing: 'Never get into a pissing match with a skunk.' Uncertain of exactly who the skunk was, Lord Dudley went home.

With the letter like an albatross around his neck, Barratt, who holds a personal decoration from the Queen of Commander of the Victorian Order, insists that it is better all forgotten. He feels it was a silly squabble between two women friends that simply got out of hand. Cornered, he agreed he was not there. He had to check the events he speaks of in the letter with people who were present by a series of telephone calls. And, he says, of course there was another side that favoured Lady Dudley. On reflection, had he included that in his letter, it might have given a more balanced view. But he is adamant that he made up no stories about Lady Dudley.

She is adamant that, presumably acting under instructions, Barratt has turned the truth on its head.

It does seem unlikely that people who work in the Diplomatic Corps and in embassies would complain to a secretary about their distinguished guests. John Barratt's letter was written less than a month after he had left the service of the Kents – presumably for his health's sake. Certainly he had had a distressing exchange with the Princess, after which she refused to speak to him, and then he had resigned in the May.

In his letter he accused Lady Dudley of making an embassy girl employee cry over a tip. The system in embassies – as, indeed, it is in any one of the Queen's homes, private and State-owned – is that guests are told how much to leave as a tip for the staff. The Queen suggests £5 a head for the footman and maid who look after a couple. The tipping is run the same way in embassies. A girl employee brings in an envelope and explains how much should be put into it. It saves a lot of heart-searching on the part of the guests.

The question is, was it Lady Dudley or was it Princess Michael who gave the girl a flea in her ear when she came with the envelope? Lady Dudley, who has been staying at embassies for many a long year, is appalled at the suggestion that she would refuse to pay. When asked what the girl should do about Princess Michael's tip, she told her she would have to sort that out with the Princess. In the normal way, it was something that John Barratt would have dealt with, had he not been in hospital.

The problem with the consul in Ohio seems to boil down to the fact that the consul was muddled about the plane time and thought they were going to be late. He rushed upstairs to hurry Maureen Dudley and barged into her room, shouting 'Quick, we are leaving now,' to find her half-undressed.

'Ow!' said Lady Dudley, reaching for a towel, amused rather than enraged, as the consul retreated in mild confusion.

One society hostess who knows both the Princess and the Countess explains the end of the friendship between the Princess and the Countess thus:

> Maureen is passionate about manners. If someone attacks her conduct, she will be formidable in her own defence.
>
> To Maureen Dudley that is what that letter was all about; an attack on her integrity. Their relationship could not have survived. Maureen did enjoy the glamour of having a Princess as her best friend and some people would have a Princess as a close friend on any terms.
>
> Maureen does not take that view. And so she disassociated herself from Princess Michael. To this day she believes that John Barratt did something that was not just unfair, but deeply dishonourable.

What, then, had inspired that letter? One thing is certain. Although Barratt will not discuss the episode, it was a phone call from his old employer that brought it about. The Princess, after enquiring how he was getting along, asked her former secretary if he would kindly set out his account of what had passed while Lady Dudley and herself were in the United States. 'I saw no reason not to set things out as I understood them,' Barratt later told friends.

It was all something of a storm in a teacup, but the repercussions still rumble on.

Chapter 8

The Future

IT WAS EITHER amazing courage or breathtaking cheek, whichever way you care to regard it, when quite unexpectedly Princess Michael turned up at the men's finals at Wimbledon on the very day that the *News of the World* broke the story of her affair with Ward Hunt. She appeared in the royal box on the centre court, wearing a pretty pale blue and white dress, arm in arm with her long-suffering but still adoring husband, and flanked by Princess Alexandra and the Duke and Duchess of Kent and their children. Ever her father's daughter, she was facing head-on a situation where she had to crush rumours and prove to the world that her marriage was working.

The centre court crowd of 14,500 gave the Kent family a standing ovation as they appeared in the box. The seating had been rearranged so that Princess Michael and her husband were visible in the front row. This had been done by the Wimbledon officials after a request was made from York House, the Kents' official London home.

Princess Michael sat in a green wicker chair surrounded by brothers- and sisters-in-law, Kent nieces and nephews. The Kent family were closing ranks in the face of the controversy.

At first Princess Michael appeared a little nervous, twisting her wedding ring, the famous smile conspicuous by its absence. Her main concern seemed to be to devote her attention to her husband. Several times she laid her head on his shoulder and grasped his hand; she even went so far as to pull gently at his beard. It was quite a performance, if somewhat over the top, and the crowd loved it. The following day, hundreds of messages of support and bouquets of flowers for the Princess flooded Kensington Palace.

The British press were more sceptical. *Private Eye* splashed its cover with the headline 'GERMAN WIMBLEDON TRIUMPH' (the young German, Becker, had won the men's singles, but this was not what they had in mind). The *Eye* ran four inside stories about the long-running Princess Michael saga. The main one of these, headed 'Love Forty', read:

> Grasping her husband firmly by his beard, the young blonde German strode onto the Centre Court to make Wimbledon history. For a moment there was stunned silence. And then the crowd exploded into a tumultuous cheer. 'God save the Princess of Michael!' they cried as the smiling Princess held up her husband for all to see. Yes, she had won.

Unfortunately, as *Private Eye* pointed out in their own inimitable way, she had overdone it. As usual.

And back at Kensington Palace there were, not unsurprisingly, reports of screaming rows, one so violent that it disturbed the peace of five of the other apartments. The Princess became nearly hysterical and later, for some reason, a chandelier had to be taken to be mended. But, nevertheless, though the marriage might have been badly dented, like the chandelier it was by no means completely broken.

For one thing, having unceremoniously dumped Ward Hunt, the Princess was determined that her position would remain unchanged. This time, she was not going to make any statements or apologies; she was just going to ride it out. And she had made it clear that, if the marriage did have to end in the wake of the scandal, she would go and take the children, Lord Frederick and Lady Gabriella, with her. This was the ultimate threat, and an unthinkable thing to happen to two royal children, both of whom are in line to the throne.

In actual fact, she was on safe ground simply because her husband believed he could not live without her. He felt that he and she were an inseparable couple, made for each other, and he was determined that the marriage would survive. Even when it began to dawn on him that there might be something wrong, he had not been able to accept it. He refused point-blank to face up to the thought that there was another man in her life, and the possibility of a break-up did not exist as far as he was concerned.

He refused to read the newspaper stories about his wife's activities; he would not listen to the radio or watch television. He tried desperately to act as if nothing had happened. He did not wish to know what she had done or what was being said. In that way, he reasoned, he could not make a mistaken remark that could be misinterpreted if he was asked questions. And, besides, the Princess had convinced him that it was all a wicked press campaign; first Robert Maxwell revealing her Nazi father, and then

Rupert Murdoch's papers making up nasty stories about Ward Hunt. Lies, all lies.

'I need my wife,' he said. 'I love her and could not face life without her. She is the mother of my children and they need her, too.'

It had been suggested to the couple by Palace advisers that it might be politic to leave England for a while – at least until the end of August – while the fuss over the Ward Hunt episode died down. With all the Princess's public engagements cancelled until the beginning of September, and their children left in the care of the nanny, on 11 July they took a flight from Heathrow under assumed names. Their staff and the airport staff were sworn to secrecy regarding their destination. 'They just want to be alone together until all the fuss dies down, and hope they will be left in peace this time,' said a member of the household. Their private secretary, Colonel Farmer, said: 'The holiday was planned several weeks ago. They wanted to be together and that is exactly what is happening.'

It didn't take too long for the press to discover where the Prince and Princess were bound. The next day, 12 July, it was revealed by all of Fleet Street that the Prince and Princess were to enjoy a luxury cruise around the Mediterranean on the 206-foot schooner *Jessica*; a vessel that cost £5 million when it was custom-built only eighteen months before and that was one of the largest sailing ships in the world.

They were certainly getting away from the fuss. Unfortunately, they were creating a new one. Their host and the owner of this splendid boat was an Argentinian and, to add to the indiscretion, an Argentinian who was reported to be an arms-dealer, one Señor Carlos Perdomo. It was said he had supplied the infra-red night-sights used by Argentinian troops during the Falklands war. These were dangerous waters for members of the royal family to sail upon and not exactly what the Palace had had in mind when they suggested a quiet period of disappearance.

But, regardless of rumblings from Buckingham Palace, the Princess had been determined on the cruise. She had met Perdomo at the Antigua party for the opening of the St James's Club in January, and his offer of sanctuary in these times of trouble had been gratefully received.

Señor Perdomo, pleased as punch to have such important guests, said that he supposed the royal couple were taking a holiday with him 'to relax, to be at peace and to rest. They are two very beautiful people who live in superb harmony.'

After two nights spent with friends on the Côte d'Azur, the Prince and Princess boarded the yacht. James Whitaker, the *Mirror*'s royal reporter, bearded them at the gangplank and thrust a copy of a newspaper report regarding their host's Falklands war activities into the Princess's hand. An unnamed major London arms-dealer had been quoted as saying: 'He [Perdomo] didn't supply any of the big stuff like Exocet missiles, only the highly technical back-up equipment such as infra-red night sights. They cost anything up to £30,000 each.'

The Princess glanced briefly at the story, said, 'We don't read that newspaper,' and walked on. But a few minutes later one of the yacht's officers came out and asked if he might have the newspaper and it was taken on board.

Mr Whitaker was then able to refute the arms-dealer story. Señor Perdomo gave him an interview and Señor Perdomo said: 'I don't supply arms to nobody. The only time I have arms is when I go shooting in Africa. Then I use them. I have never seen infra-red anything. I haven't even been in Argentina for seven years. I left my country many years ago and I don't go back.'

On board the royal couple shared one of the schooner's

four superb cabins. They had an eight-foot bed and rose early for a breakfast of grapefruit, toast and marmalade, and coffee. Then Princess Michael changed into a bikini – she had brought a different one for each day – and her husband put on his swimwear. They spent hours reading and improving their tans, sunbathing on one of the cabin roofs with Perdomo's wife and his daughter. Or she would put on stereo headphones and doze off to the music.

The royal couple would have felt quite at home with the décor of the yacht. The Señor has obviously been inspired by things British. There are deep, floral-patterned sofas everywhere, bathrooms so spacious they border on the Edwardian, and an animal-trophy room, where tusks of elephants plus the guns with which the Señor shot them decorate the walls.

There is even a fireplace complete with chimney to complete the homey atmosphere.

Jeroboams of champagne were brought aboard to be drunk with candlelight dinners of sea-food or pasta which started quietly enough at about 9.30 each night for the five people on board. But by 11.30 p.m., when they said their goodnights, the laughter was loud – with the Princess laughing loudest and longest.

Ian Bridges, one of the many drifting young men who work the boats around the Mediterranean, had landed a job as a deckhand in *Jessica*. He quit the schooner on the Friday after the Prince returned to Britain and he gave his inside story of the rift-healing cruise to the *News of the World*.

He said that there had been whispers that Prince and Princess Michael might be aboard *Jessica* weeks before they arrived. 'But my first reaction', he said, 'was to groan. All it meant to me was that the Argentinian owner, Carlos Perdomo, would demand standards on the schooner to be perfect rather than just very, very good.'

The crew were all issued with new white uniforms and

warned to be on their best behaviour. They were ordered to polish the three-masted schooner's teak and mahogany interior until it mirrored their faces. Every solid gold door-knob was buffed until it gleamed.

'I couldn't help but watch the Prince and Princess as I went about my duties as a deckhand,' Ian Bridges said.

> What I saw was a couple laughing and chatting closely, kissing, holding hands and looking as if they had very few cares. Most of the time they seemed relaxed and as if they were in love. There was only one fleeting incident that said something about the pressure they must have been feeling inside.
>
> They were alone on the main deck when I heard him shout something like: 'Blast it. I thought you'd packed that shirt I like.'
>
> It took me aback because he was always so mild mannered and now he was angry over a shirt. The Princess kept cool and said: 'No, darling. I don't think I did.' Then there was an awkward silence for a few minutes as they sat, side by side in their deckchairs staring out to sea.
>
> We all agreed that she has an unintentional way of making you feel she's flirting a bit when she talks to a fellow. She laughs a lot, and thought it was very funny when her white sunhat blew overboard. The Prince only left her side to windsurf or swim. Riding the waves is his favourite sport. He is very good at it and he would disappear for long stretches when we dropped anchor in bays.

The couple rarely went ashore as they wanted to avoid publicity, and each time *Jessica* sailed the crew were given twelve different ports where she might be anchoring next.

'In fact,' said Ian, 'the couple only felt free to walk about when we pulled into the secluded Corsican bay of Calvi the day before the Prince was due to return to Britain. They spent an hour or so there, wandering about the little town, and came back smiling.'

On his last morning, the Prince was sad to be leaving and the Princess went ashore with him in a wooden long-boat and then went by car with him to his private jet. He kept glancing at her very wistfully, and she looked tearful as he said: 'Goodbye, my darling, you know I shall miss you.'

Soon after she got back to the boat he was waving farewell again – from the sky. The Prince had ordered the pilot to bank steeply so that he could get a final glimpse of the Princess where she was watching his departure from the deck of the schooner.

Prince Michael was returning home to fulfil three public engagements. He attended a meeting of the Royal Patriotic Fund, of which he is president, in the morning, and in the evening he took the salute at the Royal Tournament. He took with him his son, Lord Frederick, and a party of ten schoolfriends. That engagement was followed by a charity banquet at Hampton Court which the Princess had been due to attend with him.

One significant detail that Ian Bridges had missed from his watch on the royals was the visit of a German cousin of Prince Philip, who had been sent down to the south to talk to the couple. He had instructions to tell them that the Queen would not tolerate any more scandals and wanted a full reconciliation between the couple. She had also sent a message asking the Prince to stay away with his wife for a longer period. But the meeting ended in a bitter argument, with the Princess storming out and refusing to continue the discussion. The Prince flew home, as he had originally planned to do, the following day.

The Princess was not moping after her husband left. She was spotted that night at Palma's exclusive Club de Mar, smiling as widely as ever. And *Jessica* had a new guest – Prince Alfonso Holenlohe, who once caused a society scandal by marrying the sixteen-year-old Princess Ira Furstenberg.

Jessica was steaming to Marbella and a vast party to be thrown by Adnan Khashoggi. Surprisingly, Princess Michael flew home early, missing an extravagant evening of the kind which is normally meat and drink to her. Why? one wonders. Was she truly missing Michael? Or was it because Khashoggi happens to be one of Laura's, Mrs Ward Hunt's, greatest friends?

She left the boat at Marbella, took a taxi to Malaga airport, and the Prince met her at Heathrow. She had travelled alone. They drove straight to Kensington Palace in a black Ford Escort sports car, with no detectives, no fanfare, and no comment. 'They are delighted to be together again,' said a friend. 'And don't expect to be parted for some time.'

Funny, that, because on 15 August, three weeks later, Prince Michael caused more speculation by flying off to Palma, Majorca, to stay with another wealthy friend, diplomat Ivan Ivanovic. He flew under the assumed name of Mr Edwards on a routine package-flight holiday from Gatwick airport. The *Sunday People* newspaper rang Nether Lypiatt Manor where the Princess was staying with her children and a woman who said she was the house-keeper answered the call. She was a remarkably chatty housekeeper.

'This trip is rather like the Prince sailing at Cowes, one which he always takes alone,' she explained. 'He'll be back from his holiday next week and the Princess will be there to meet him. It really amounts to nothing more than that. Like many couples, the Prince and Princess follow many pursuits of their own within their private relationship. There's really nothing more to it than that. It's just an annual holiday that he takes with the boys.' The house-keeper also added: 'This is an annual holiday he has undertaken without the Princess for the past three years. He takes this holiday at the same time every year.'

The Princess had nothing to do but wait. She stayed at

home in the country and the one engagement she did have never happened. She was to greet the Virgin Atlantic *Challenger* at Hamble when the boat arrived after crossing from New York. *Challenger* sank.

The Prince returned earlier than expected on Wednesday, 21 August. He had been sent word that his wife was depressed and he quite literally flew to be at her side. He was also, in time, to practise for a horsey event that was to be held at Sandringham the following weekend. He came back to find that the Princess might have been depressed, but she had something important to tell him. She confirmed her original decision; the Ward Hunt affair was truly over. She was genuinely shaken by the exposure she had received and was subdued, and had been quietly working on her book with her secretary Anne Frost.

The royal family were all at Balmoral. The Michaels of Kent were not invited.

Then went together to the World Horse and Carriage Driving Championships at Sandringham. The Prince competed in the pairs championships on one of the Queen's horses. He picked up 8.5 penalty points on his round.

Prince Philip did come to the carriage-driving event, but he completely ignored Princess Michael, though he chatted briefly to her husband. Stung by the snub, behind the scenes the Princess gave her husband hell, a local journalist discovered later, though publicly the united front was maintained. They were photographed together, she pressing against his shoulder and leaning towards him, smiling, of course, and wearing a soft wool hat with a turned-back brim. Very much the country girl.

Her own friends – and it is true to say that there are few of them – are wondering if she herself would be wise to remain with Prince Michael. She is likely to be an outcast from the royal family for many years, and the freeze began quickly after the scandal erupted. She was not invited to the 1985 garden-parties at the Palace, she was not asked to be present while the Falklands Commemoration Stone was set, and she was invited to Ascot for only one day of the four-day meeting. And on that day she had other fish to fry with Ward Hunt in the Cotswolds, and Prince Michael joined the Queen's party alone. She was not in the royal party at Rupert Murdoch's Hampton Court Palace party to celebrate the bi-centenary of *The Times*. The rest of the royal family were, and if Murdoch's papers had been printing 'lies, all lies' it seems strange they would honour the event with their presence. She was not asked to the State Opening of Parliament. She talks of retiring from public life, perhaps as a face-saver. It's unlikely to happen.

But, still, she is experiencing the same freeze that the Earl of Harewood shivered through after his divorce. He broke the royal rules and from then on was barred from all royal occasions, including Princess Anne's wedding and the funeral of the Duke of Windsor. The Queen values family life above all else and has a horror of divorce and the events that lead to it. And it is said that she was appalled by the incontrovertible evidence of the Ward Hunt affair that the *News of the World* presented. It would have been surprising if she hadn't been. Scandal is something that the royal family go to any lengths to avoid. Princess Michael will certainly pay the price for her indiscreet behaviour.

As autumn moved towards winter, the Prince and the Princess appeared to be beginning to lead separate lives, making few joint appearances.

Prince Michael went on an important visit to Wales on 18 October. The Welsh were delighted with the charming, hard-working Prince, and they probably would have loved the Princess had they been given the opportunity to see her. But Prince Michael went alone.

Just nine days later, on a Sunday evening, he was alone

again at a friendly charity function mounted by the Celebrities Guild. Ella Glazer, the Guild's organizer, had enquired if the couple would be free to attend. Ella Glazer was delighted that the Prince agreed to present awards to 'Unsung Heroes' but a shade disappointed that the Princess could not be there with him. Kensington Palace had not been certain whether the Princess was free that evening, and suggested it would be better to opt for just the Prince.

At the beginning of November, the royal couple were apart again. The Prince was on a brief but hectic business trip to Munich, reinforcing his role as a royal ambassador for British business.

Back home, Princess Michael was looking ahead and considering her own future. She had an enterprising idea; a plan to present a series of television programmes on the stately homes and castles of Britain. She considered that a tie-up with the millionaire producer and television director David Frost might get the series off the ground.

She was realizing that she needed some different and more sympathetic exposure if she wanted to return to the public life that she so enjoys. A serious project that would cancel out the terrible publicity she had lived through in her fortieth year. The presentation of an erudite series taking her via the small screen into millions of homes was perhaps the answer.

And her financial problems become more pressing every day. What family treasures that can be taken quietly to Sothebys for private sale have already gone. There is a limit, even among the very richest, to financial gifts and help in return for friendship with royalty. And the friends the Princess makes therefore can only become more and more questionable. There are quiet but well-founded rumours that even her bank is anxious about the size of the overdraft.

Someone who knows her well commented that she was the most avaricious person she had ever met. She said:

'It's all money with her. Although she basks in the style and dignity and title of Princess, if she found someone with sufficient money she would probably go. Hunt didn't have enough for her.'

She does try to earn money, and one of her possible sources of income is as an after-dinner speaker. She has already attempted this, and successfully. Her maiden performance took place at a Vienna conference of a British computer company, ICL. She handled her speech with ease and talked of self-motivation and some of Europe's princesses who had left their countries for greener fields. It has been said she asks and gets about £2000 for an appearance. Australia's chief head-hunter for after-dinner speakers, Christine Maher of Celebrity Speakers, tried to tie up a contract with the Princess but was told that the Princess prefers to deal directly with clients and was not in the habit of paying commission.

There is also the book about princesses for Weidenfeld, for which she is supposed to have been paid a £10,000 advance. The project seems to have struck a dead end. Her main researcher was her mother's cousin, Countess Kate Szapary, a hospital wardsmaid who died in January 1985 while the Prince and Princess were in Antigua. Although the Princess was close to the Countess, she did not return for the funeral, saying that royalty never attended funerals. But since the scandal broke she has been working on the book project again.

She made a surprise and unwise appearance on television to talk about the fabric designer Laura Ashley after Mrs Ashley died following a fall down a flight of stairs at her daughter's home. On a sad occasion, the famous smile never once left her face. It was a 'look at me' performance in the worst possible taste. The television company declined to say how much she had been paid for the appearance.

And in September, with amazing nerve under the circumstances, she lobbied for the civil-list question to be raised again. She grumbled that the Duke of Kent, Princess Alexandra and the Duke of Gloucester all contribute less than she and Prince Michael do, yet they receive respectively £127,000, £120,000 and £94,000 a year. To some extent she does have the royal family over a barrel in that they cannot demand she cease to take presents when she receives no income from 'the firm' as Prince Philip calls the royal family. But the point she cannot grasp is that she is not obliged to contribute; she does it because she enjoys the limelight and the prestige, so the suggestion that the Queen should provide an annual allowance from her private purse is likely to go unheeded.

Yet her outgoings are enormously high. At the height of her popularity she received over a thousand letters when one of her beloved cats disappeared. Public sympathy was such that she might have lost a child, and every letter was replied to. It costs money. She complains that her telephone bills are in the region of £5000 a year, and she employs a girl secretary as well as Anne Frost, plus more temporary helpers when the pressures of work become too great.

The country house with its swimming-pool, tennis courts, children's playground and enclosed formal gardens must cost a fortune in upkeep. She hunts with the Beaufort and the Cotswolds, which means stables to run. It's not surprising she does most of the cooking herself to save the expense of a chef. And it seems that even Nether Lypiatt Manor's ghost that welcomed her so warmly has deserted her. Recently the Princess called in an exorcist.

And, to add to their financial troubles, Prince Michael has lost one of his better perks. His directorship with STC gave him the loan of a chauffeur. Unfortunately, with business economies in the autumn of 1985 and a new chairman – Lord Keith in place of Sir Kenneth Corfield – the use of the chauffeur was withdrawn. It was a post that the Kents could not afford to finance themselves, and it was a considerable blow. As it is, their domestic staff consists of daily women.

By late September she was putting a cautious toe in the water and beginning to appear in public again. In her 'exile' she had taken a leaf from the Prince and Princess of Wales's diet book and cut down on meat, butter and fried foods. She lost 20 lb in weight, and spent most of the summer riding and playing tennis to get in shape. She is riding in eventing competitions for the Talland team, and Aitken Hume, of which her husband remains a director, sponsor her horse-box.

In October she grabbed all the headlines at her first major public appearance since Ward Hunt was sent packing. It was a fashion gala, held by the Italian designer, Gianni Versace, at the Victoria and Albert Museum. One has a vision of the royal family picking up their morning papers to see photographs of the Princess posing with models Jerry Hall and Marie Helvin and sighing: 'There she goes again.'

She appeared in a slinky black dress with pearl drop earrings and her now much shorter hair piled on top of her head. She looked stunning, beaming for the photographer and, unlike your average member of the royal family, freezing as she saw a camera aimed in her direction.

Journalist Noreen Taylor watched her performance with a steely eye and wrote with an acid pen:

> Like the instinctive actress she is, she knows the value of a lovey-dovey shot of her and the Prince.
>
> 'Be nice for them, darling,' she says to her still bewildered husband. So he just stands there next to her.
>
> Boring shot, so she turns, plucks a flower and hands it to him with lots of hand brushing and coy eye contact.

> Picture over and he is still standing there feeling
> a right Wally with the flower in his hand. A breezy
> Versace aid rescues him by pinning the flower to
> his lapel.
>
> Now it's time to circulate. 'Dreamy' seems to be
> Princess Michael's favourite word.
>
> The flowers are 'so dreamy'. Your dress is 'a
> dream'. Your hat is 'a dream'.
>
> Prince Michael looks as if he's having a bad
> dream.

Yes, the British press's love-affair with Princess Michael is definitely over.

And before she went to the show she lunched with Michael Szell, a bachelor fabric designer, at San Lorenzo in Beauchamp Place. They spent two hours over an Italian lunch, and a *Sun* photographer captured their departure – she leaning back against Mr Szell, her head just not quite on his shoulder, her eyes gazing soulfully into his and the smile exchanged for a look of deep meaning. It wouldn't have been surprising if people had said they were in love.

But, back with her husband, they both attended a Gala Charity Concert for the Blind at London's Royal Festival Hall. Marie-Christine was beginning to creep back into the limelight.

Perhaps one of the many quotes from her which most reveals how she sees herself was given for an Australian television documentary. She was speaking of family life and her children.

> They haven't realized yet that I am not like other
> mummies. I was leaving for a fancy dress ball in a
> crinoline, tiara and Prince of Wales feathers in my
> hair – frankly I felt like the sugar plum fairy.
>
> Ella said: 'Mummy, you look like a Princess.' 'But
> Mummy is a princess,' I told her. My husband and
> I fell into each other's arms.

But it is not quite enough to have the title in the British royal family. There are obligations that go with the role.

She also once said that whenever she goes on a public appearance she says a little prayer. It goes: 'Dear Lord, please don't let me make a gaffe.'

Poor Marie-Christine. It seems that for her God doesn't often listen.

MC chose her own path and the road from Waverley to Windsor has been long and hard and strewn with egg shells. She hasn't been careful in treading over them and these days the Castle's drawbridge isn't lowered to let her in. How long the situation lasts is in the hands of the lady herself.

Though she managed to pick plenty of beautiful rushes as the boat glided by, there was always a more lovely one that she couldn't reach.

'The prettiest are always farther!' she said at last, with a sigh at the obstinacy of the rushes in growing so far off.

Index

Act of Settlement (1701), 12, 92
Adlerstein, Hans von, 46
Airlie, Earl of, 85
Aitken, Timothy, 119–24, 124
Aitken Hume Bank, 95, 120, 185
Albert, Alexis, 48–50
Albert, Elsa, 48–50
Albert, Ted, 48–50, 54, 57
Alexandra, Princess, 14, 86, 93, 107; marries Angus Ogilvy, 69; advises Prince Michael, 75; children, 79, 109; Prince Michael's wedding, 81, 89; at Wimbledon, 171–2; civil list, 184
Alice, Princess, see Gloucester, Duchess of
d'Alpuget, Blanche, 39
Amies, Hardy, 81
Anne, Princess: Prince Michael's wedding, 81, 119; children, 109; riding, 112; marries, 181
Anson, Lady Elizabeth, 121
Armstrong, James, 132
Ashley, Laura, 183
Atkinson, Dr Michael, 91
Attila the Hun, 37

Banda, Dr Hastings, 121
Barchard, Betty, 111
Barker, Charles, 60
Barratt, John: Mountbatten's private secretary, 74; Princess Michael's secretary, 97, 98–101, 158–9; illness, 158, 160, 161; and the Dudleys, 164, 166–70
Barry, Stephen, 105–6
Bayoud, George, 135
Becker, Boris, 172
Bowie, David, 97
Bridges, Ian, 176–7, 178
Brooks-Baker, Harold, 128
Brown, Monsignor Ralph, 89–90, 91, 92
Buddenbrock, Rosemary von, 41

Caroline of Monaco, Princess, 134
Cartland, Barbara, 101
Catherine of Castille, 36
Cats, 159
Charles, Prince of Wales, 63, 111, 150; relations with Princess Michael, 13, 102, 104; girlfriends, 67; marriage, 76; criticizes Church, 83; Kensington Palace, 94,

Charles, Prince of Wales –
    contd.
    102, 105; and Emanuels,
    102–3; roof garden, 105;
    children, 109
Chauvel, Elyne, 30
Chauvel, Sir Harry, 30
Chiavelli, Dr Marino, 145
Christoper August of Hesse,
    Prince, 129
Churchill, Winston, 87
Coggan, Dr Donald, 76, 77
Colefax & Fowler, 61
Corfield, Sir Kenneth, 184
Courcy, Anne de, 44, 59–60,
    69–70, 88
Cowles, Fleur, 157–8
Crone, Ida, 22–3

Daily Express, 71
Daily Star, 151
Dallas, 133
Dallas Times Herald, 134
Debrett, 128
Dekyvere, Mrs Marcel, 45
Dempster, Nigel, 146, 165
Diamond, Neil, 133
Diana, Princess of Wales:
    marriage, 76; and Eman-
    uels, 102–3; relations with
    Princess Michael, 104;
    children, 109
Dorothea of Hesse, Princess,
    49
Dougherty, Patrick, 66–7
Driver, Ronald, 113, 144
Dudley, Earl and Countess
    of, 153–70
Dudley, Lady Susanna, 158

Edward VIII, *see* Windsor,
    Duke of

Eichstedt, Baron Hugo von,
    22–3
Elizabeth, the Queen Mother,
    13, 86, 108, 111, 121
Elizabeth II, 49, 64, 128, 168,
    180, 181, 184; attitude to
    divorce, 11–12, 72; permis-
    sion for Prince Michael's
    marriage, 11, 17, 77; mar-
    ries Prince Philip, 76; affec-
    tion for Prince Michael, 77,
    94; religious question, 80,
    81; relations with Princess
    Michael, 105, 108, 110,
    126, 156; children, 109;
    dogs, 111; Trooping the
    Colour, 112; and Princess
    Michael's background, 124
Emanuel, David and Eliza-
    beth, 102–3
English National Opera, 131–
    2, 141
Esra of Hyderabad, Princess,
    106–7, 139, 141, 142

Fairbanks, Sir Douglas, 159
Fairbanks, Mary Lee, 159–60
Fairstar, 50–1
Farmer, Col. Michael, 120–5,
    146, 148, 149, 152, 174
Fisher, Alan, 102
Foot, Michael, 77
Francisco, Chico, 139
Francisco, Magrit, 20, 118–19
Francisco, Olga, 139
Franz Josef, 36
Freeman, Verla, 151–2
Frost, Anne, 107, 146, 180
Frost, David, 182
Furstenberg, Princess Ira, 178

Galbreath, John, 145–6, 160

George I of Greece, 108
George V, 63, 93, 108, 109
George VI, 93, 108
Glazer, Ella, 182
Gloucester, Duchess of, 62, 64, 108
Gloucester, Duke of, 63, 108, 184
Goering, Hermann, 21, 22, 26, 30
Goldsmith, Lady Annabel, 150
Goodman, Lord, 156
Goronwy-Roberts, Lord, 77
Grace of Monaco, Princess, 158
Grahame's Bookshop, 38-9
Gross, Mr and Mrs Jenard, 132
Guys and Dolls, 102

Hagman, Larry, 133
Hall, Jerry, 185
Hall, Dr Philip, 117, 128
Harewood, 6th Earl of, 108
Harewood, 7th Earl of, 72, 132, 181
Harewood, Lady, 72, 132
Harfield, Mick, 55-6
Haslam, John, 150
Heim, Archbishop Bruno, 76, 79, 89
Heinrich, Prince, 134
Helvin, Marie, 185
Henri II, 36
Henri IV, 37
Heseltine, Michael, 105-6
Himmler, Heinrich, 22, 28-9
Hitler, Adolf, 19-26, 61, 118, 126, 129
Holenlohe, Prince Alfonso, 178
Home, Lord, 24

Home, William Douglas, 24
Howard, Lady Mary Fitzalan, 107
Hume, Basil, Cardinal, 76, 89
Hunt, J. Ward: relationship with Princess Michael, 131-52, 171, 173, 174, 180-1; first meeting, 133; business interests, 133; divorce, 134-6; in London with mother, 136; in California with Princess Michael, 138-40; secret visit to London, 140-52, 180-1; plans to marry Princess Michael, 144; hasty departure, 148-50
Hunt, Laura, 133, 134-6, 179
Hunt, Nelson Bunker, 133, 137
Hyderabad, Nizam of, 139

ICL, 183
Ivanovic, Ivan, 179

Jessica, 152, 174-9
John of Gaunt, 37
John Paul II, Pope, 89, 90
Jones, Anthony Armstrong, *see* Snowdon, Lord
Jones, David, 38
Junot, Philippe, 134

Karl of Hesse, Prince, 49
Keith, Lord, 184
Kent, Edward, Duke of: father's death, 74; advises Prince Michael, 75; Prince Michael's wedding, 81, 89; marries Katherine Worsley, 84-5; inheritance, 93;

Kent, Edward, Duke of –
  contd.
  Freemasons, 143; at Wimbledon, 171–2; civil list, 184
Kent, George, Duke of, 74, 84, 86, 87, 108
Kent, Katherine, Duchess of, 84–5, 86, 171–2
Kent, Marina, Duchess of, 77, 84–6, 87, 93, 108
Khashoggi, Adnan, 134, 179
Kleinwort Benson, 61, 73
Knatchbull, Amanda, 76
Konrat, Col. Georg von, 23, 29
Kruger, Mrs Aaron, 132

Lay, Mimi, 133
Levin, Bernard, 161
Lightbody, Donald, 142
Linley, Viscount, 13, 97
Lodge, Mr and Mrs Morton, 34–5
London United Investments, 95, 144
Lowenstein, Prince Rupert, 143
Lyon, Elizabeth Bowes, *see* Elizabeth, the Queen Mother

MacDonald, Marie, 46
Maher, Christine, 183
Mail on Sunday, 153–4, 155, 156
Majesty, 68–9, 74, 87–8, 103–5
Mapp, Graham, 55, 56
Margaret, Princess, 94, 97; divorce, 11–12, 72; relations with Princess Michael, 13; advises Prince

William, 63; children, 110; and Earl of Dudley's poem, 155
Marina, Princess, *see* Kent, Marina, Duchess of
Mary, the Princess Royal, 85, 108
Mary, Queen, 63, 86, 108
Maxwell, Robert, 174
Meder, Marie, 27–8
Menzies, Robert, 44
Michael of Kent, Prince: 'invisible Prince', 11, 97; Queen's permission to marry, 11, 17, 77; forfeits place in succession, 12, 75, 80; in Australia with Princess, 54–7; first meets Marie-Christine, 62–3, 77–8; army career, 63, 94, 96; dinner in Brussels, 65–7; girlfriends, 67; courage, 67–8; horsemanship, 68–70, 180; motorcycle, 71; death of father, 74, 86–7; Mountbatten advises, 74–7, 93, 95, 97–8, 100, 101, 111; Queen's affection for, 77, 94; humour, 77–8; wedding, 78–83, 119; honeymoon, 83–4; children, 80, 91–2, 102, 109, 121, 133, 149, 173, 178, 186; church blessing, 89–92; inheritance, 93; shortage of money, 93, 94, 99, 131, 184; death of mother, 93; Kensington Palace, 94; Nether Lypiatt Manor, 95; directorships, 95, 96, 119, 184; ancestry, 108–9; in Antigua, 113, 136–7, 183;

Princess's television interview, 120-1; in Texas, 131-4, 137; Freemasons, 143; Princess's 'nervous breakdown', 147, 149, 150; in Ohio, 157-60; at Wimbledon, 171-3; marital strain, 173-4; Mediterranean cruise, 174-8; separate lives, 178, 179, 181, 182; 'a bad dream', 186

MICHAEL OF KENT, PRINCESS: relations with royal family, 11-12, 13, 102, 104, 105, 110, 180, 185; Queen's permission for marriage, 11, 77; character, 12, 14, 99-100, 106, 182-3; self-promotion, 12, 41, 47, 113-14; lack of money, 12, 45, 93-6, 98-9, 182-5; nicknames, 13, 35, 40, 47, 68, 95; physique, 13, 39; public duties, 13, 96-8; 'anywhere for a hot dinner', 13, 131; popularity with public, 14, 125, 184; fantasies, 14-15, 40-4; HRH, 15, 77; birth, 19, 29; ancestry, 19, 31, 36-7, 49, 53, 61; early years in Australia, 30-1, 33-50; education, 36-40, 59-60; horseriding, 37, 68-70, 111-12, 185; Grahame's Bookshop, 38-9; and 'Carolines', 38-9, 45; dressmaking, 38, 47; dieting, 39, 185; in Africa with father, 40-4; social ambition, 44, 48; charity committees, 44-5; Catholic faith, 45, 71-4, 76, 78-83, 88-92; at J. Walter Thompson, 46-8, 66; and Ted Albert, 48-50, 54, 57; travels to Europe, 50-2; Vienna, 52-3; interior designer, 53, 59-60, 99; returns to Australia, 53-7; arrives in London, 53; charm, 55, 111; at Charles Barker, 60-1; accent, 60, 103; at Colefax & Fowler, 61; Szapar Designs, 61; marriage to Tom Troubridge, 61-7, 71-4, 79; meets Prince Michael, 62-71, 77-8; and Prince William, 63-7; dinner in Brussels, 65-7; annulment, 71-4, 91; children, 72, 73, 80, 91-2, 102, 109, 121, 133, 149, 173, 178, 186; Mountbatten advises, 74-7, 93, 95, 97-8, 100, 101, 111; papal objections, 78-83, 88-9; marries Prince Michael, 78-83, 119; honeymoon, 83-4; 'foreignness', 87-8; church blessing, 89-92; and civil list, 94, 99, 184; Kensington Palace, 94-5, 105-6; Nether Lypiatt Manor, 95; *folie de grandeur*, 96, 101, 106-7, 160; gaffes, 101-2, 187; roof garden, 105-6; cats, 111; in Antigua, 113, 136-7, 183; father's Nazi past, 115-29, 174; TV-am interview, 119-24, 125; cries in public, 126; and J. Ward Hunt, 131-52, 171, 173, 174, 180-1, 185; 'nervous breakdown', 145-

MICHAEL OF KENT, PRINCESS
– *contd.*
51; and the Dudleys, 153–
70; and John Warner, 155,
162–6; book on princesses,
167, 183; at Wimbledon,
171–3; marital strain, 173–
4; Mediterranean cruise,
174–9; separate lives, 178,
179, 181, 182; television
plans, 182; tribute to Laura
Ashley, 183
Mirror, 102, 115–29, 175
Mitchell, Tom, 30, 34
Mitford, Unity, 24
Montagu of Beaulieu, Lord,
90
Montgomery, David, 150,
151–2
Morgan, Hugh, 78
Mountbatten, Earl, 74–7, 93,
95, 97–8, 100, 101, 111
Murdoch, Rupert, 174, 181
Mussolini, Benito, 129

Negroponte, Diana, 70–1, 73
Neville, Lord Rupert, 128
News of the World, 117, 138,
140–52, 153, 155, 171, 176,
181
Nicholas of Greece, Prince
and Princess, 109
Nicholas II, Tsar, 19, 36, 53,
109
Norfolk, Duchess of, 107
Norfolk, Duke of, 107
Northampton, Marchioness
of, 141, 143, 144
Northcott, Sir John, 49

Ogilvy, Hon. Angus, 14, 69,
85, 109, 119
Ogilvy, James, 79

Ogilvy, Marina, 79
Olga, Grand Duchess, 108
Osborne, Susan, 65
Owen, Nick, 122

Paul VI, Pope, 80, 90
Pearce, Sandy, 47
People, 179
Perdomo, Señor Carlos, 174–9
Peters, Clarke, 102
Philip, Prince, 109, 184; re-
lations with Princess Mi-
chael, 13, 113, 180; mar-
riage, 49, 76; German
relatives, 128–9, 178
Philippa of Portugal, 36
Phillips, Davina, 67
Pinching, Evie, 59, 157
Pond, John, 46
Principal, Victoria, 133
Private Eye, 172–3

Reagan, President Ronald,
138
Redesdale, Lord, 24
Rees, Merlyn, 77
Reibnitz, Frederick von, 27,
37, 40, 44, 56–7
Reibnitz, Baron Gunther
von: marries Marianna
Szapary, 19; first wife, 20;
member of Nazi party and
SS, 20–9, 115–29; friend-
ship with Goering, 21, 26;
Jewish blood, 22–3; ancestry, 22–3; religion, 26, 27,
28; insults Himmler, 28;
'punishment unit', 29; re-
joins cavalry, 29; expelled
from party and SS, 28, 29;
flight, 30; divorce, 30; in
Africa, 30, 40–4; reunited

with Marie-Christine, 40–4; her wedding, 82, 119; Nazi past revived, 115–29, 155; Lebensborn, 126; denazification court, 127–8

Reibnitz, Magrit von, *see* Francisco, Magrit

Reibnitz, Marianna von, *see* Rogala-Koczorowski, Countess

Richard of Gloucester, Prince, 64

Robertson, Mrs Constance, 48

Rodgers, Sherren, 157

Rogala-Koczorowski, Countess: ancestry, 19; marries von Reibnitz, 19; skiing, 24; distrusted by Gestapo, 24–5; divorce, 30; in Australia, 30–1, 33–50, 56; remarries, 36; grandson, 109; and husband's Nazi past, 116, 123, 125, 130

Rogala-Koczorowski, Mathias, 36, 56, 125

Rogala-Koczorowski, Count Tadeusz, 36, 56

Roosevelt, Franklin D., 86

Rossington, Norman, 102

Rowlands, Sir James and Lady, 55

Royal Marriages Act (1772), 77

Royal Secrets (Barry), 105–6

Ruark, Robert, 42

Savary, Peter de, 113, 136–7

Savoy, House of, 36

Scheer-Tross, Margherita, 20

Schmauser, Obergruppen-führer, 28

Schuette, Esther, 41

Scott, Sir Peter, 81, 100

Seward, Ingrid, 68–9, 74, 87–8, 103–5

Shea, Michael, 115–16, 117, 118, 119, 120

Sheldon, Bob, 77

Silverman, Jerry, 157

Simpson, Wallis Warfield, *see* Windsor, Duchess of

Siveright, Pammy, 112

Smith, Bill, 134–5

Snowdon, Lord, 11–12, 63, 72, 94, 95

Sophie of Greece, Princess, 129

Standard Telegraph and Cables, 184

Starkloff, Zsusui, 63–4

Stassinopoulos, Ariana, 161

Stein, Marion, 72

Stellenwerck-Frampton, Mrs Brooke, 134

Stern, Der, 117

Sun, 125, 186

Sunday Telegraph, 59

Swartzenburg, Prince Frederick, 53

Sydney Morning Herald, 48

Szapar Designs, 61

Szapary, Countess Kate, 183

Szapary, Count Lazlo, 51–2

Szapary, Marianna, *see* Rogala-Koczorowski, Countess

Szapary, Countess Yvonne, 49

Szell, Michael, 186

Talland, 185

Taylor, Elizabeth, 155, 162, 163

Taylor, Noreen, 185–6

Texas Business, 134–5
Thatcher, Mark, 134
Thomas, Dylan, 95
Thompson, J. Walter, 46, 66
Times, The, 103, 181
Tomkinson, Charles Palmer, 63
Troubridge, Sir Peter, 62
Troubridge, Tom, 61–7, 71–4, 79
Tubman, President, 64
Tuckwell, Patricia (Bambi), *see* Harewood, Lady
TV-am, 119–24, 125

Under Milk Wood (Thomas), 95
Universe, The, 90–1

Valin, Reg, 60–1
Van Pollen, 60
Versace, Gianni, 185
Villiers, Sir Charles, 70
Villiers, Diana, *see* Negroponte, Diana
Virgin Atlantic *Challenger*, 180

Wafik Said, 107
Walbrook Investments, 95
Ward, Jeanne, 136
Warner, John, 155, 162–3, 165, 166
Warwick, Christopher, 103–5
Webber, Andrew Lloyd, 159
Weidenfeld, Lord, 167

Weiner Library, 126
White, Mrs, 132
Whitaker, James, 102, 118, 175
Wiesenthal, Simon, 127
Wiessler, Nana, 126–7
William of Gloucester, Prince, 62, 63–7, 74
Williams, Sir Max, 154, 156
Wilson, Sophie, 55
Windisch-Graetz, Prince, 25
Windisch-Graetz, Prince Frederick, 49
Windisch-Graetz, Princess Hedwig, 19
Windsor, Duchess of, 13, 79, 83–4, 86
Windsor, Duke of, 79, 83–4, 86, 108, 181
Windsor, Lord Frederick, 91, 102, 109, 133, 149, 173, 178
Windsor, Lady Gabriella, 91, 102, 121, 133, 149, 173, 186
Windsor, Lady Helen, 81
Wolfson, Patricia, 67
Woman's Weekly (Australia), 41
Worsley, Katherine, *see* Kent, Katherine, Duchess of
Worsley, Sir William, 84–5
Wran, Neville, 55
Wright, Sir Oliver, 161

'Zoke', 151–2